Prepare for the
Great Tribulation
and the Era of Peace

Volume LXI:
(Volume 61)

October 1, 2010 – December 31, 2010

by

John Leary

Queenship
PUBLISHING COMPANY
P.O. Box 220 • Goleta, CA 93116
(800) 647-9882 • (805) 692-0043 • Fax: (805) 967-5133
www.queenship.org

Dedication

To the Most Holy Trinity

God

The Father, Son and Holy Spirit

The Source of

All

Life, Love and Wisdom

Cover art by Josyp Terelya

Library of Congress Number # 95-73237

Published by:
    Queenship Publishing
    P.O. Box 220
    Goleta, CA 93116
    (800) 647-9882 • (805) 692-0043 • Fax: (805) 967-5133
    www.queenship.org

Printed in the United States of America

ISBN: 978-1-57918-401-4

Acknowledgments

It is in a spirit of deep gratitude that I would like to acknowledge first the Holy Trinity: Father, (Jesus), and the Holy Spirit; the Blessed Virgin Mary and the many saints and angels who have made this book possible.

My wife, Carol, has been an invaluable partner. Her complete support of faith and prayers has allowed us to work as a team. This was especially true in the many hours of indexing and proofing of the manuscript. All of our family have been a source of care and support.

I am greatly indebted to Josyp Terelya for his very gracious offer to provide the art work for this publication. He has spent three months of work and prayer to provide us with a selection of many original pictures. He wanted very much to enhance the visions and messages with these beautiful and provocative works. You will experience some of them throughout these volumes.

A very special thank you goes to my spiritual director, Fr. Leo J. Klem, C.S.B. No matter what hour I called him, he was always there with his confident wisdom, guidance and discernment. His love, humility, deep faith and trust are a true inspiration.

Equal gratitude also goes to our prior spiritual advisor, Father Donald McCarthy, C.S.B.

My appreciation also goes to Father John V. Rosse, my good pastor who is retiring from Holy Name of Jesus Church. He has been open, loving and supportive from the very beginning.

There are many friends and relatives whose interest, love and prayerful support have been a real gift from God. Our own Wednesday, Monday and First Saturday prayer groups deserve a special thank you for their loyalty and faithfulness.

Finally, I would like to thank Bob and Claire Schaefer of Queenship Publishing for providing the opportunity to bring this message of preparation, love and warnings to you, the people of God.

John Leary, Jr.

Declaration

His Holiness, Pope Urban VII states:

In cases which concern private revelations, it is better to believe than to not believe, for if you believe, and it is proven true, you will be happy that you have believed, because our Holy Mother asked it. If you believe, and it should be proven false, you will receive all blessings as if it had been true, because you believed it to be true. (Pope Urban III, 1623-44)

The Catechism of the Catholic Church states:

Pg. 23, #67: Throughout the ages, there have been so-called 'private revelations,' some of which have been recognized by the authority of the Church. They do not belong, however, to the deposit of faith. It is not their role to improve or complete Christ's definitive Revelation, but to help live more fully by it in a certain period of history. Guided by the Magisterium of the Church, the sensus fidelium knows how to discern and welcome in these revelations whatever constitutes an authentic call of Christ or His saints to the Church.

Publisher's Foreword

John has, with some exceptions, reported receiving messages twice a day since they began in July, 1993. The first of the day usually takes place during morning Mass, immediately after he receives the Eucharist. If the name of the church is not mentioned, it is a local Rochester, NY church. When out of town, the church name is included in the text. The second occurs in the evening, either at Perpetual Adoration or at the prayer group that is held at Holy Name of Jesus Church.

Various names appear in the text. Most of the time, the names appear only once or twice. Their identity is not important to the message and their reason for being in the text is evident. First names have been used, when requested by the individual.

We are grateful to Josyp Terelya for the cover art, as well as for the art throughout the book. Josyp is a well-known visionary and also the author of *Witness* and most recently *In the Kingdom of the Spirit*.

Early in 1999 John's bishop established a special commission to read John's published works and to talk to him about his religious experiences. The commission rendered its report in June. By letter of June 25, 1999 John was advised to have an explanatory note printed in the front of each book. This note appears on page xi of this edition.

Fr. Frederick W. Bush is John's new spiritual advisor, and he has reviewed the messages beginning with Volume 56.

Previously the messages were being reviewed by Rev. Donald McCarthy, C.S.B., who was John's spiritual advisor. He has retired due to medical reasons.

This first edition under these rules has resulted in a delay of 90 days.

Late in October, 1999 John Leary and Carol were called to the office of the Diocese of Rochester for a meeting with the Vicar General. The result of the meeting was that they (the Diocese) are now allowing John to publish under their obedience. John was cautioned against mentioning the subjects called to John's attention in the bishop's original declaration (see page ix). John was further ordered to have his spiritual advisor read and approve each book. This is being done on each book.

This volume covers messages from October 1, 2010 through December 31, 2010. The volumes have been coming out quarterly due to the urgency of the messages.

Volume I: July, 1993 through June, 1994.

Volume II: July, 1994 through June, 1995.

Volume III: July, 1995 through July 10, 1996.

Volume IV: July 11, 1996 through September 30, 1996.

Volume V: October 1, 1996 through December 31, 1996.

Volume VI: January 1, 1997 through March 31, 1997.

Volume VII: April 1, 1997 through June 30, 1997.

Volume VIII: July 1, 1997 through September 30, 1997.

Volume IX: October 1, 1997 through December 31, 1997.

Volume X: January 1, 1998 through March 31, 1998.

Volume XI: April 1, 1998 through June 30, 1998.

Volume XII: July 1, 1998 through September 30, 1998.

Volume XIII: October 1, 1998 through December 31, 1998.

Volume XIV: January 1, 1999 through March 31, 1999.

Volume XV: April 1, 1999 through June 13, 1999.

Volume XVI: July 1, 1999 through September 30, 1999.

Volume XVII: October 1, 1999 through December 31, 1999.

Volume XVIII: January 1, 2000 through March 31, 2000.

Volume XIX: April 1, 2000 through June 30, 2000.

Volume XX: July 1, 2000 through September 30, 2000.

Volume XXI: October 1, 2000 through December 31, 2000.

Volume XXII: January 1, 2001 through March 31, 2001

Volume XXIII April 1, 2001 through June 30, 2001

Volume XXIV July 1, 2001 through Sept 30, 2001

Volume XXV October 1, 2001 through December 31, 2001

Volume XXVI January, 2002 through March 31, 2002

Volume XXVII April 1, 2002 through June 30, 2002

Volume XXVIII July 1, 2002 through September 30, 2002

Volume XXIX October 1, 2002 through December 31, 2002

Volume XXX January 1, 2003 through March 31, 2003

Volume XXXI April 1, 2003 through June 30, 2003.

Volume XXXII July 1, 2003 through September 30, 2003

Volume XXXIII October 1, 2003 through December 31, 2003

Volume XXXIV January 1, 2004 through March 31, 2004

Volume XXXV April 1, 2004 through June 30, 2004

Volume XXXVI July 1, 2004 through September 30, 2004

Volume XXXVII October 1, 2004 through December 31, 2004

Volume XXXVIII January 1, 2005 through March 31, 2005

Volume XXXIX April 1, 2005 through June 30, 2005.

Volume XXXX July 1, 2005 through September 30, 2005

Volume XLI October 1, 2005 through December 31, 2005

Volume XLII January 1, 2006 through March 31, 2006

Volume XLIII April 1, 2006 through June 30, 2006

Volume XLIV July 1, 2006 through September 30, 2006

Volume XLV October 1, 2006 through December 31, 2006

Volume XLVI January 1, 2007 through March 31, 2007

Volume XLVII April 1, 2006 through June 30, 2007

Volume XLVIII July 1, 2007 through September 30, 2007

Volume XLIX October 1, 2007 through December 31, 2007

Volume L January 1, 2008 through March 31, 2008

Volume LI April 1, 2008 through June 30, 2008

Volume LII July 1, 2008 through September 30, 2008

Volume LIII October 1, 2008 through December 31, 2008

Volume LIV January 1, 2009 through March 31, 2009

Volume LV April 1, 2009 through June 30, 2009

Volume LVI July 1, 2009 through September 30, 2009

Volume LVII October 1, 2009 through December 31, 2009

Volume LVIII January 1, 2010 through March 31, 2010

Volume LIX April 1, 2010 through June 30, 2010

Volume LX July 1, 2010 through September 30, 2010

Volume LXI October 1, 2010 through December 31, 2010

The Publisher

Readers Please Note:

Bishop Matthew H. Clark, Bishop of Rochester, has accepted the unanimous judgment of a special mixed Commission set up to study the writings of John Leary. After reading the volumes and meeting with Mr. Leary, they testified that they found him psychologically sound and spiritually serious. They concluded that his locutions are not a fraud perpetrated on the Catholic community. Nevertheless, in their judgment, his locutions are of human origin, the normal workings of the mind in the process of mental prayer.

Of grave concern to the Bishop and the Commission, however, are the errors that have found their way into his writings, two of which are most serious. The first is called by the Church millenarianism. This erroneous teaching, contained in the first 6 volumes of *Prepare for the Great Tribulation and the Era of Peace,* holds that Christ will return to reign on the earth for a thousand years at the end of time. As the *Catechism of the Catholic Church* expresses it:

> The Antichrist's deception already begins to take shape in the world every time the claim is made to realize within history that messianic hope which can only be realized beyond history through the eschatological judgment. The Church has rejected even modified forms of this falsification of the kingdom to come under the name millenarianism ... (CCC #676).

The second error is anti-papalism. While the Church holds that the Pope by reason of his office as Vicar of Christ, namely, as pastor of the entire Church, has full, supreme and universal power over the whole Church (Vatican II, Constitution on the Church, #22), Mr. Leary's locutions select Pope John Paul II to be obeyed but his successor to be ignored as an imposter pope. This erroneous teaching is found in all the volumes.

Because Mr. Leary has reaffirmed the teaching and discipline of the Church and acknowledged the teaching authority of John Paul II and Bishop Matthew H. Clark and their successors, Bishop Clark has permitted these volumes to be published with this warning to its readers appended.

Visions and Messages of John Leary:

Friday, October 1, 2010: (St. Therese of Lisieux)
At St. John the Evangelist after Communion I could see St. Therese not only as she came to me, but I could see her talking to Paul. St. Therese said: *"My dear son, I am happy to greet you again, and to help you in your mission. I know that you have many responsibilities in your earthly*

1

duties and your spiritual duties, but Our Lord has reminded you several times that it is so important to do your minimum prayer time. My prayer time with Jesus was always a joy, and much more desirable than my earthly duties. At times you may feel pressured to do so many things, but it is important to keep peace in your soul and carry out your tasks as time permits. Do not overburden your day with more things than you have time to accomplish. Always limit your objectives to something that is achievable, and do not worry about something that you did not have time to do. Be able to ask Jesus to discern what are the most important tasks to do first. If others try to change your discernment of order, just tell them that it is on your to do list. Getting frustrated at what to do first, or how to find enough time to do everything, should not cause you to lose your peace. Make the best discernment, and do what is needed most. You will never accomplish everything, so do not let the evil one try to rush you and upset you. I pray for you in your mission, so call on me in your needs with prayer.”

Later, at the Divine Mercy Holy Hour at Holy Name I could see the same people at morning Mass and at the holy hours. Jesus said: *“My people, My daily Mass people and My faithful adorers at Adoration are the core of My prayer warriors that I depend on the most for prayers and evangelization. These are My special souls that will have a great treasure in heaven for all of their hours of Masses, rosaries, and Adoration. These souls have a deeper love relationship with Me every day. Once you go beyond your duty of Sunday Mass, you truly are called to share all of your life with Me in your daily troubles and activities. I want My faithful to keep your focus on Me in loving Me and helping your neighbor out of love for Me. When you give your will over to Me in all that you do, then I can use your work to save more souls. Give praise and glory to Me every day, even as My angels and saints give Me homage in heaven every day. The closer you come to Me, the more you are preparing for your life with Me in heaven.”*

Saturday, October 2, 2010: (Guardian Angels)
At St. John the Evangelist after Communion I could see a young child with her guardian angel standing beside her. Mark said: *“I am Mark and I stand before God. You remember in Scripture when the Lord came to the prophet in a whisper. This is also how you need to be quiet to hear my prompting to do good things. You are also in some dangerous*

physical environments at times where I am looking out for your safety. You also need to avoid occasions of sin in some temptations in flipping through channels of your TV and also on the internet. Guard your eyes also from dwelling on sinful thoughts. When you are on your way to your talks, I am also with you to help you arrive on time. Thank you for praying for my help in your morning prayers. I am always at your side for advice and spiritual help, so call on me whenever you are having difficulties in life."

Later, at St. Theodore's tabernacle I could see several church steeples in every small town. Jesus said: *"My people, every town has at least one church and the old churches could be found by looking for a tall steeple. You are seeing a decline in Sunday Mass attendance in many parts of America. There is a process going on that could have many contributing factors, but the main problem is that people are becoming lukewarm in their faith. First you see a closing of your Catholic parish schools. Then you see clusters formed of neighboring churches. This is finally followed by closing some of the clustered churches. Part of this problem is that the parishioners are not being spiritually fed by just a ten minute homily every Sunday. People have become so lazy in their faith, that they get upset if the homily is any longer than ten minutes. To truly feed My people, you should be hearing a half hour sermon that could teach My people more about the basics of the faith. A sermon is a teaching experience, while a homily is just a rewording of the readings, and not always an application to your daily lives. By spending more time to teach everyone the basics of the faith, then coming to Mass would be more inspiring. Many Catholics are going to Protestant groups that preach a lot longer than ten minutes. Once you truly understand the basics of your faith, you would not desire to give up My Eucharist to attend another church. My priests and bishops need to build up the people's faith, or you will see your attendance at Mass get even worse."*

Sunday, October 3, 2010: (Right to Life Sunday)

At Holy Name after Communion I could see a merry-go-round with many young children on it, and it was right in front of a magnificent church that was all in gold. Jesus said: *"My people, this vision of the many children on a merry-go-round, is symbolic of how many more children that could be in My Church if it were not for your abortions*

and birth control. Think of all the lives and missions that I had planned for your people, but now they will not be fulfilled because of your convenience and selfishness. Many souls desire the pleasure of their lust, but they do not want to face up to the consequences of an unexpected pregnancy. Some of these abortions come from sexually active young girls who are not ready to bring up children, but there are also abortions from affairs of adults, and even married people. Whether abortions are performed for convenience or out of embarrassment, they are still grievous sins against My plans for human life. It is this taking of life, and the disrespect for life that is weighing heavily against America. These sins continue, and My justice will also be demanded when you are called to account for these sins. Just as My babies had to pay a dear price in the loss of their lives, so America will have to pay a dear price when your freedoms and your possessions are taken away from you. You make gods out of possessions, wealth, sports, and fame, and because you worship these things before worshiping Me, I will take all of these things away from you as you will suffer in exile. Your country needs to wake up and stop murdering My babies with your abortions, or you will be sealing America's fate."

Monday, October 4, 2010: (St. Francis of Assisi)
At St. John the Evangelist after Communion I could see some women being brought up in an open elevator which represented souls being raised up in the levels of heaven after their judgment. Jesus said: *"My people, I have encouraged My faithful to be perfected and work on their spiritual lives to attain heaven. Even beyond the minimum to gain heaven, you can work harder to strive for the higher levels of heaven. There are spiritual riches and joys that are the reward for those who bring many souls to heaven. The more effort that you make to do My Will on earth, the greater your reward will be in the higher levels of heaven. In the vision you are seeing souls graduate to the higher levels of heaven after their judgment. The closer that you come to Me in our love relationship with your devotions, good works, and saved souls, the closer I will bring you to Myself in the higher levels of heaven. My faithful will rejoice when I show them their reward for all of their earthly suffering and their hard work for Me. The more of your pains, sufferings, and striving to do My Will which you offer up to Me, the more treasure that you will have stored up in heaven. When you arrive in heaven, your*

peace, love, and joy in My beatific vision will be complete in My love for you."

Later, at St. Theodore's tabernacle I could see a rich looking building where the heads of state were having secret meetings of how to run the world's economy. Jesus said: "*My people, these secret meetings are planning the demise of America so you can be taken over through your debts. The one world people are bringing down the value of the dollar, which is why gold, silver, and your other commodities have higher prices in dollars. As a country continues running deficits relative to its worth in GDP, the value of that currency will decrease as there is more of a chance for default on its debts. If you were to chart your budgets in the United States over the last ten years, you could see how your deficits are rising at a rate that you cannot afford to pay even the interest. The interest is becoming a larger portion of your budget and you gain nothing from paying it off. This debt problem is forcing your budget to shrink on other needed items because the capital is also being taken out of your corporate needs to borrow. If America cannot eliminate its deficits, you could soon see a bankruptcy coming that would cause chaos and riots in your streets when your entitlements would cease. This will be one of the causes of your coming martial law, that will be the end of your country as you know it. When this occurs, you can call on Me and I will have your guardian angel lead you to the nearest refuge of protection. Pray for My help to protect your souls and your body from being killed by the evil ones.*"

Tuesday, October 5, 2010:

At Holy Name after Communion I could see a bus taking travelers to their destinations. Jesus said: "*My people, back in the days of St. Paul most of their transportation was focused on horses and ships. He was a strong-willed missionary to bring souls to Me after his conversion. Considering his limited transportation abilities, he traveled a lot as you can read in his writings. Today, My disciples and messengers have airplanes, cars, and the internet, along with books and DVDs to spread My message of the Kingdom of God. With all of these means at your disposal, there is even more of an obligation to take advantage of these gifts to help evangelize souls. As the tribulation time approaches, the Antichrist will also take advantage of your means of communication to try and force people to worship him. This is why I have told you after the Warning to remove your televisions, computers, and radios from your homes so you do not look at the Antichrist's eyes or listen to his voice. Refuse to take his chip in your body, even if the evil ones threaten to kill you. Also, refuse to use smart cards, or cell phones once he is declared because his voice will control you like a robot. Once you see him about to come into power, you need to call on Me to have your angel lead you to the nearest refuge of protection so you will be free from the Antichrist's control and from any attempt to kill you."*

Later, at St. Theodore's tabernacle I could see a night skyline of a city and there were lights along the coast. Then I saw a picture of Santa Claus as somebody handing out money to people. Jesus said: *"My people, as a result of your recession and your corporations sending most of the manufacturing jobs out of the country, you now have high unemployment with little chance of these lost jobs returning. As long as cheap imports are allowed to steal your markets, America cannot compete without a level playing field. The less good paying jobs that are available, the lower your average income will be for each family, even with two working. With so many people on unemployment insurance, welfare and food stamps, this puts stress on the state and local governments where less taxes are being collected. More people are being included below the poverty line because of scarce jobs, and lost jobs are also causing more home foreclosures. It is difficult to have peace of mind when many are hurting financially with their household incomes barely able to pay their bills. Some are looking more to local food shelves just to have enough food to eat. Those, who are better off, could help the poor with donations to food shelves, or providing jobs. When the tribulation comes, you all will be trusting in My protection and relying on Me to provide for your food and shelter. Some of these hard times are preparing people to live without their possessions and comforts. Pray for My help both now and when you will be at your refuges."*

Wednesday, October 6, 2010: (St. Bruno)
At Holy Name after Communion I could see the Early Church in its struggle over circumcision from the Jewish custom. Jesus said: *"My people, there have been certain disagreements over parts of the faith with various heresies over the years, but I have guided My Church through these rough waters. In the Early Church there was a disagreement on*

7

whether new converts had to be circumcised or not as a Jewish custom. Later, this requirement was dropped. Then in the Middle centuries there was a division and a break away of the Eastern Rite church. Martin Luther started another major rift in the Church which resulted in Protestant sects that did not follow the Pope. The Anglican Church was another split because of King Henry VIII. It is unfortunate that Christian believers have become so divided over the years because of certain belief differences. As you are approaching the end times, there will be even a further division in My Roman Catholic Church between a schismatic church and My faithful remnant. The schismatic church will be preaching New Age which is not even a religion of God. This church will also be teaching that the sexual sins are no longer mortal sins. My faithful remnant will follow My apostolic teachings, and this branch will be My Church protected from the gates of hell. Do not be taken in by any heretical teachings of modernism or New Age. If you see this in your church, then work to change it. If you cannot get it changed, then leave that church for a faithful remnant church that teaches My true Word. Pray for discernment from the Holy Spirit to direct you in keeping your traditional faith."

Later, at St. Theodore's Adoration I could see trees and their leaves were changing color. Jesus said: *"My people, when you see the leaves changing color and falling, the nights getting longer, temperatures getting cooler, and more rain, these are the signs of the fall season coming. Just as you are observant of the seasonal changes, so you also need the eyes of faith to see that the end times are coming as well. When you see people losing their faith, the evil ones planning a takeover by the Antichrist, chips in the body being forced on people, and preparations for your death camps, you can read these signs of the coming tribulation. I have enabled people to set up refuges to protect My faithful remnant during the tribulation. You will need to have full trust that My angels will protect you by making you invisible to the evil ones. You will need to leave your homes at the proper time, but fear not because I will provide for your food and lodging. When you see the Antichrist come into power, know that My victory is near. You will be living your purgatory on earth, but you know that the Antichrist's reign will be short. Pray to have the strength which you will need to bear your cross in this evil time."*

Thursday, October 7, 2010: (Our Lady of the Rosary)

At St. John the Evangelist after Communion I could see someone praying the rosary. Jesus said: *"My people, when you pray the rosary, it is your special time with Me in praying for all of your petitions. This feast day was in honor of My Blessed Mother's protection of Europe from the invading Muslim ships that were defeated in a storm at sea at the Battle of Lepanto. My Blessed Mother has given you her rosary of fifteen decades as a daily prayer for your help and protection. Some think this is too long to pray, or it is just an old tradition, but the rosary is a powerful weapon against evil and its forces. When you call on us in prayer, your prayer petitions are always heard, and I will answer them in ways that benefit the most souls. You pray your rosaries daily, especially for My Blessed Mother's intentions. The four intentions that you were given are for the souls of poor sinners, the souls in purgatory, for peace in the world, and for the stoppage of abortion. You have family members who may be away from Me, and your prayers for them need to be persistent, since their souls may demand a heavy price to be saved. Pray for what is best for these souls in leading them to heaven. Saving souls is your most precious calling, and prayer is the best way to bring your petitions to heaven."*

Later, at the Eternal Father prayer group at Holy Name Adoration I could see Obama campaigning for office and he had a stage with a black curtain. After his election, he opened the black curtain to reveal his socialist left agenda that he was going to force on all of us. Jesus said: *"My people, your current administration has used your recession as an opportunity to spend trillions of dollars on his own agenda which has not helped the job situation even after two years. This agenda is more about government control of banks, the car industry, and the health industry. Government jobs are not permanent or productive, which is why you have problems in all parts of your business world because of government interference. Pray that your elections can help correct this takeover agenda."*

I could see some statues of Our Lady's appearances at various apparition sites. Mary said: *"My dear children, at almost every apparition site I have asked you to pray my rosary for all the troubles and evils in your world to stop. I thank all of you for praying my holy rosary on this feast day of the Holy Rosary. You have many intentions which I am giving over to my Son, Jesus. Have faith and trust that your prayers will be answered according to my Son's will in His time."*

I could see the rafters of a house in the basement, and there was a considerable amount of water in the basement. Jesus said: *"My people, there are many people under water where their mortgage is much more than the true value of the house itself. Several banks have put a freeze on selling foreclosed homes because they will lose money to auction them off at reduced prices from the mortgages that they hold. This interference with market prices could cause major problems with your housing industry. Pray that a fair arrangement can be made to deal with foreclosed homes."*

I could see many election campaigns focused on the high deficits and the high unemployment rate. Jesus said: *"My people, it is obvious to many investors and other world governments that America is overspending beyond what she can afford. Your mounting deficits are about equal to your GDP and you remember the problems Greece had when its debts were too high. The dollar is losing its value because of these debts that are too high. This is seen in your increased commodity prices of gold, silver, and oil. If this spending cannot be contained relative to your collected taxes, then America is headed for bankruptcy and hyperinflation. Pray that your representatives will come to their senses and make cuts where it is necessary."*

I could see a focus on the ceiling of a room. Jesus said: *"My people, every year your Congress has to vote on the ceiling of your National Debt. In the past this has been raised at outrageous increases, but this needs to be the first place to stop the runaway spending. Your taxes both on property and on income should also have some reasonable ceilings based on what people can afford to pay. Your entitlements, public pensions, and your debts are all out of control, and they need to be reined under control to what taxes are collected, and they should be relative to other workers' pay and benefits. Without some control over these expenses, your government will not be able to afford these outlays. America needs to control its spending before you see a collapse in your money system."*

I could see scandals in the workings of the large banks that were bailed out. Jesus said: *"My people, as more investigations are making public the murky workings of your banks, it is being revealed how they sold junk quality bonds on suspect houses, and made derivative bets against them. When home backed securities became toxic, some banks profited from insurance companies as AIG when the banks had insured their bets against their bonds. AIG was bailed out by the taxpayers and they paid even foreigners for the hedge bets against these bonds. This control of the banks and derivatives by the one world people is how they intend to bankrupt your government. Be prepared to go to My refuges*

11

when this crash and takeover begins."

I could see a continuing fruitless war continuing in Afghanistan. Jesus said: *"My people, many of your wars are promoted by the one world people, and these same people are instrumental in starting them. These wars are linked to your Defense Industrial complex which needs wars to justify its existence. Many American and foreign lives are being lost with no clear reason for the U.S. remaining in this war. The reasons for starting this war were planned, but there is no benefit from winning. Instead, pray for peace and stop getting involved in useless wars that last a long time."*

I could see the need for more prayer for peace and some problems in the world finances. Jesus said: *"My people, many people are suffering financially and you do not need unnecessary wars and killing to add to it. You can see the one world people bringing about their plans for a world takeover and leading up to the Antichrist's reign. The problems that you have today are nothing compared to the tyranny of evil that will come in the tribulation. Pray for your spiritual and physical protection that I will bring in the protection of My refuges. You are in a battle for souls and this is more important than losing your possessions and comforts."*

Friday, October 8, 2010:

At St. John the Evangelist after Communion I could see a clock going around and in the background there was a Mass being said in a private home. Jesus said: *"My people, this clock speeding up in the vision is showing you that in the near future you will see the religious persecution increase so much that the priests will have to offer Mass underground at secret Masses in the homes. Home Masses will only go on for a short time as the tribulation will soon follow and all of My faithful will need to go to My refuges for protection. This is when you could encourage your priests to come with you to the refuges. Even if you cannot have a Mass at My refuges, My angels will bring you daily Communion and you will have tabernacles to adore Me at your refuges as well. I will always be with you even through the worst of the coming evil days. Trust in Me for all of your needs as My angels will defend you from the evil ones."*

Later, at St. Mary's Adoration, Denver, Co. I could see some faithful protesting abortions at a Planned Parenthood abortion clinic. Jesus said:

"My people, those, who support abortion and even promote abortion, are sinning against the lives of My babies. To vote for a candidate that openly supports abortion, is also an action that supports abortion and is liable to My judgment. People, who hold office and vote for bills that support abortion, also are liable for a priest to refuse them Communion if they do not repent. My people should avoid voting for candidates who support abortion because their apparent disdain for life even questions their moral judgment in other areas. This is not just a one issue decision, but it indicates a support of a death culture that is running America. Your media people criticize some honest candidates who are even against abortion in rape and incest cases. These babies from such cases are still innocent lives, but these same media people are not critical of all the innocent millions of babies being slaughtered. You need to be consistent in your decisions to support life in all instances. Do not let the death culture candidates get away with lying about the truth of My Word. Stand up and defend these babies from those who want to kill them. Call the doctors and mothers murderers for their abortions. I will accept their repentance, but they need to ask for My forgiveness to be saved. Whenever you can stand up and protest the taking of life in abortion, do so in front of the clinics who perform abortions for blood money. If you do not stop your abortions, America will face its own demise."

Saturday, October 9, 2010:

At St. Mary's Church, Denver, Co. after Communion I could see some nuns praying and the one nun was carrying a gavel as she was atoning for sin because of the justice of God. Jesus said: *"My people, I have told you before that nations are responsible for their actions and their sins. This is why I have asked My people to pray for poor sinners and to make reparation for the sins of your country. This is a mission for the cloistered nuns as in the vision. The gavel that the nun was carrying, represents how they are praying to mitigate My justice against America's sins. You know that there is a price for everyone's sins, and the more prayers and offerings that are given up to Me, the easier it will go for each soul. There is a balance of sin and evil with prayer and good deeds. So when the evil gets worse than those who are praying, then My justice must be carried out against that nation. This again is why I depend on My prayer warriors, and if you miss your rosaries one day, then you need to make them up the next day."*

Sunday, October 10, 2010:

At St. Mary's Church, Denver, Co. after Communion I could see Naaman cleansing in the Jordan River to heal his leprosy. Jesus said: *"My people, in two of today's readings you read of how people were miraculously healed of their leprosy. In the one case Naaman was healed by the prophet Elisha, and in the Gospel ten lepers were healed by Jesus. In addition to physical healings, there were also spiritual conversions. In the vision in the river there is a representation of Baptism as St. John the Baptist baptized many by immersion in the water. When people are blessed with My gifts, it is unfortunate that not everyone is quick to thank Me as the Samaritan did. You have many things to give Me thanks for in your gift of faith, your gift of life, and your loving relationship with Me, especially in My Eucharist. Some should be grateful for a good marriage, children, and grandchildren. Others have been blessed with a job, food to eat, and a home to go to. You take many things for granted such as the air you breathe, the light from the sun, and water to drink. It is when you are without these gifts that you may more fully appreciate their value to you. When you have droughts, floods, or loss of electricity, you appreciate your proper amount of water, and the ability to have your electrical appliances work. So give praise and thanks to Me for all that you have through Me. You can show your appreciation by sharing your gifts with others, and you will be storing up your reward in heaven. Your family and friends are gifts to each other, so share your love with them and all those who are a part of your life."*

Monday, October 11, 2010:

At the Shrine of St. Therese Adoration, Pueblo, Co. I could see a small shrine that housed a scene of the Nativity. Jesus said: *"My people, in a month or so you will be preparing for another Advent Season leading up to the celebration of My birth on Christmas. Even some of your merchants are already stocking their stores to sell gifts for Christmas. In the Gospel reading I told the people that no sign will be given except for the sign of Jonah. Jonah called on the people of Nineveh to repent of their sins or the town would be destroyed. These people did repent in sackcloth and ashes, and their lives were spared. In a similar manner My messengers are calling on My people to repent of their sins as well, but only a few are listening and praying. When I was born, you saw a sign in My star over Bethlehem, and the shepherds and Wise men followed the star to Me. Now in these days, you have My Scriptures giving you signs of when I will come again to the earth in splendor on the clouds. One sign is that evil will increase, and another sign is that the people will become lukewarm in their faith. Other signs will be in the increased earthquakes and pestilence in viruses afflicting your people. You will see famines and a division in My Church. You will also witness a major sign in My Warning experience that will wake up many sinners. As these things happen, I will send a sign when it is time to leave your homes for My refuges of protection. When you see the Antichrist come to power, know that soon I will be coming to claim My victory over the evil ones."*

At the refuge property: Jesus said: *"My people, this arid land is much like the desert of the Exodus. I showed you the water and the antelopes on the very land itself. Whatever refuge buildings that are made, more will be multiplied. Whatever food you have, will also be multiplied. Trust in My help and My angels for those who are called to prepare refuges for My people."*

Tuesday, October 12, 2010:

At the Shrine of St. Therese, Pueblo, Co. after Communion I could see Jesus suffering and bleeding on the cross and then the cross slowly disappeared. Jesus said: *"My people, your priest asked why I had to suffer a crucifixion and die on the cross for My people. I could have chosen other means to redeem sinners, but I love mankind so much that I wanted to suffer to show you My great love. I also wanted to offer up My Blood sacrifice to wash away your sins. The offerings of animals has nothing to do with humans. I became a man and died for you also to fulfill Scripture that promised mankind a Redeemer. By one man, Adam, sin came into the world, and by one man in Myself, sin has been conquered and I have atoned for all sin both in the past and in the future. I give every soul an opportunity for redemption, but all souls have to make a personal choice to accept Me into their lives and believe in Me to be saved. By loving Me and your neighbor as yourself, you are open to be received in heaven. By your good deeds and actions you will be judged worthy of the Lamb to enter into eternal life with Me in heaven. By eating My Body and drinking My Blood in Holy Communion, you will have eternal life with Me. Come to Me all who are burdened with this life, and I will give you eternal rest for your soul. For My yoke is easy and My burden is light."*

Wednesday, October 13, 2010:
At St. Theodore's Adoration I could see some apartment buildings and a large green serpent was engulfing them. I also saw a pyramid representing Mason involvement. Jesus said: *"My people, this serpent engulfing apartments represents how evil people were involved in writing mortgages for overpriced homes for people who could not afford these homes. When these dwellings were not being paid for, the banks or creditors sold these mortgages to Fannie Mae and Freddie Mac who now control them, as they have added five trillion dollars of liability on the taxpayer as part of your National Debt obligations. These toxic assets were absorbed by the government, and they are still financing mortgages. Many people are in foreclosure and some banks are not foreclosing or allowing properties to be auctioned off at a loss. Some are leaving their homes because the house is now worth much less than the original mortgage. Others have lost their jobs, or some had their payments raised beyond their ability to pay the whole mortgage. Such foreclosures are adding more inventory of houses to be sold, and the condition of these homes are causing home prices to fall. Credit to buy houses has become more difficult to obtain and there has been a decrease in houses sold both new and old. These conditions are causing turmoil in the housing industry. Many people also have lost money on the bonds that used these houses for collateral. Once the foreclosures started, then these bonds and derivatives became junk bond status that no one wanted to buy. This was a created crisis because the creditors knowingly sold mortgages to those people who they knew would not be able to pay for them. Pray that the common man can find a proper settlement so he does not lose his investment in his home because of fraudulent bankers and creditors."*

Thursday, October 14, 2010: (St. Pope Callistus I, martyr)
At Holy Name after Communion I could see a cave where the Early Christians hid to protect themselves from being killed. Jesus said: *"My people, in the first three hundred years after My birth, it was very difficult for My early followers even to admit that they were Christians.*

Christians were killed or martyred for their faith if they were discovered. This is why many in Rome hid in the catacombs for protection. The Popes as well in this time faced martyrdom. The Early Christians hid in caves and had their Masses offered in secret caves as well. This time of persecution of My followers will again be coming during the tribulation. The evil ones will be seeking out religious people to kill them, just as in this early period after My death. You will again have to have secret Masses in the homes. As the persecution grows worse, you will need to call on Me to have your guardian angels lead you to the nearest refuge, where My angels will protect you from being killed by a shield of invisibility. These refuges will be at places of My Blessed Mother's apparitions, places of holy ground of My Eucharistic Adoration, monasteries, and even caves as in the vision. This age of the evil Antichrist will last for a short time before I will vanquish him and all the evil ones into hell. Then I will renew the earth and bring My faithful into My Era of Peace. You will rejoice in My victory over evil and the joy of My Presence."

Later, at the Eternal Father prayer group at Holy Name Adoration I could see a focus on the back door of a building as a way to enter unseen at night. Jesus said: *"My people, I am showing you the back door of a home at night because as the persecution starts, you will meet at your prayer groups secretly. By coming in the dark of night to the back door with your car parked down the road, you can still pray together without drawing attention to your meeting places. You may also wish to meet at alternate members' homes so the neighbors do not notice a pattern. This will avoid some persecution, but eventually you will need to go to My refuges for protection."*

I could see some beautiful flowers on the altar to give glory to God's creation, but even they are vulnerable as you saw the vase tip over. Jesus said: *"My people, thank you for bringing these beautiful flowers to honor Me and My Blessed Mother. I sense a hint of an evil attack as you saw one of the vases tip over. Every time you do something for My glory, there are going to be attacks as you have seen with audio recordings and TV taping. Even if you see such attacks, do not be upset because the evil one's attacks must mean that you are reaching souls to help them."*

I could see the children and wives of the miners that were trapped in a mine explosion. Jesus said: *"My people, your world has witnessed a miracle in that all the miners were able to be rescued from a deep mine in the earth. Various drilling and rescue equipment came from various countries to rescue the thirty-three miners in Chile. This was a beautiful reaching out of various nations. Everyone was very patient while the proper drilling finally located the miners. Keeping these men alive is a tribute to all those involved. This will be a beautiful display of prayers answered that all the miners were rescued. Give praise and thanks to Me that all went well for these men who endured such a long time in the dark. Coming into the light is how graced you are to see Me."*

I could see another scene in West Virginia where the outcome for some trapped miners was not as successful. Jesus said: *"My people, every rescue of miners is not always completely successful. In some cases only one or a few are rescued. You have seen many die in mines, especially in China. In such disaster cases it is not uncommon that they were a result of careless techniques and even violations of safety. These deaths result in penalties for the operators and better safety procedures. In other words some deaths could have been prevented if good safety procedures were followed and violations were fixed. Pray for the safety of these miners that they will be protected in the future."*

I could see an infant playing and an older person being cared for. Jesus said: *"My people, young children and elderly people need care givers when it is difficult to move around or when little ones need feeding and care day after day. Both old and young people put major demands on the family for time of care and even expenses for medicines and food. Daycare and nursing homes become quite expensive if needed, which is why it is better to have family help where possible. When you care for another person, hopefully you will receive some reward in your heart that makes you feel that your efforts were appreciated."*

I could see how much care was needed for an infant and an older person. Jesus said: *"My people, as you see how much care is required to help a newborn child reach maturity, you see now how much you need to thank your parents for what they endured for you. Even be thankful if you have children to help you in your old age as you helped your parents. In all cases of care giving, it takes love from the heart to carry out your mission for people. I see all of these struggles and My care givers are truly going to receive their reward in heaven. Even as you help someone who requires your help, you have a warm feeling*

*in your heart that you could contribute to someone's comfort in their
need. Pray for your care givers as much as you do for the patients."*

I could see people who had lost their houses to a fire and others who
had no heat or electricity in the winter. Jesus said: *"My people, you
have seen people in your family or close friends who may need to use
your house to live in until their houses can be repaired or the power
restored. You have lost electricity to ice storms and the like, and you
have been thankful to have backup sources of heating for yourselves
and your family. Sometimes you may have to take in your older children
until they can get a job to fix their debts. Be open in your hearts to help
those in need, even if it is just for a few days. Again, your reward for
helping family or neighbors will be great in heaven."*

Friday, October 15, 2010: (St. Teresa of Jesus, Avila)

At St. John the Evangelist after Communion I could see people coming from the darkness into the Light and they were walking on a floor
with a design of a king's crown. Jesus said: *"My people, I have been
preparing My faithful for the coming darkness of evil in the tribulation of the Antichrist. Some will be martyred, while the rest will be at
My refuges of protection. At a certain point in time, I will bring My
Comet of Chastisement to rid the evil ones on the earth during the
Three Days of Darkness. Just as the miners came out of the darkness
into the light, so in the vision you are seeing My people come out of
this darkness into My Era of Peace to greet your King in the Light of
My glory. Many people have waited patiently to be rewarded for their
faithfulness throughout the tribulation. This coming time will give you
hope for all that you are suffering now because you will soon witness
My Victory."*

Later, at St. Theodore's tabernacle I could see scientists in biological
hazard labs making viruses for germ warfare. Jesus said: *"My people, I
have warned you in previous messages how the one world people want
to reduce the population drastically down to only 500 million people
from 6.8 billion people. The quickest way to do this is to use deadly
viruses or toxic compounds in the air and water. These could be spread
by chemtrails or a simultaneous release of germs from all the germ labs
all across your country. The tip off that this is about to take place, will
be when all of your important people go underground for protection. I
will warn My people when the evil ones are about to kill a lot of people,*

so you will have time to get to My refuges and be protected from any airborne diseases. The viruses that they use will only have a short life-time, then those, who they want killed, could be removed to start over. The evil ones will have vaccines so they will not be killed. Once the population is thinned out, and they cannot find any more Christians to kill, then the Antichrist will have his short reign. In less than 3 ½ years I will then bring My own plagues and chastisement on the evil people as they will all be cast into hell. Those faithful at My refuges will be brought into My Era of Peace and be rewarded for being true to Me."

Saturday, October 16, 2010: (St. Margaret Mary Alacoque)
At St. John the Evangelist after Communion I could see evil and killings going on, and then there was a great dawn of a bright sun that cleansed everything. Jesus said: *"My people, I have prepared you for the harsh reality of the coming persecution of the tribulation. This will be an evil that you have never seen before. There will be martyrs, but many of My faithful will be protected at My refuges. This great dawn of Light in the vision is when I will bring a supernatural intervention of My victory over the evil ones. My angels will bring plagues against only the evil ones. This will be the dawn of My Era of Peace when I will bring down a new heavens and a new earth, and all the evil ones will be cast into hell. This will be a time of great joy for My faithful remnant as they will have their reward for being faithful to Me. Have no fear of the coming evil because My victory is not far off."*

Later, at Holy Name Nocturnal Adoration I could see a beautiful gold monstrance with the Blessed Sacrament inside. Jesus said: *"My people, during the tribulation there will be tabernacles and monstrances at every refuge. I have also asked My people to set up around the clock Adoration hours so I will always be with you in My Blessed Sacrament. Adoring Me and praying to Me will prepare you for the day when you will come to heaven. I have even told you to have a traveling monstrance so you can share My Real Presence with various refuges that you will visit. Just like you travel around to various churches on Holy Thursday, so you will be traveling to multiple refuges guarded by My angels. These visitations will lift the spirits of the faithful at My refuges when you come there. Be joyful that My angels will give you daily Communion if you cannot have a Mass. At My refuges you will have spiritual Manna of My Real Presence, which is better than the physical manna of the old Exodus."*

Sunday, October 17, 2010:

At Holy Name after Communion I could see some flowers coming up out of the darkness of a hole. Jesus said: *"My people, you have seen the miners being brought up out of a deep mine in Chile by a miracle drilling. This life of men coming back to their loved ones is a sign of the vision with the flowers coming up out of a hole. This coming to life again can also be seen on a spiritual level. When you live in mortal sin without confessing your sins, you are in the darkness because your soul is dead to Me. It is only by conversion by a miracle of grace or by prayers of your relatives that a soul can be brought back to spiritual life in My grace. Once your soul is again blessed with My grace and made clean of your mortal sins by absolution, then you will have rest in My love. Your constant seeking for peace can only come through Me, when you are satisfied in My rest. Keep close to Me in your daily prayers, and you will have My protection from the temptations of the devil. Treasure My love, and you will not desire to offend Me in any way by your sins."*

Monday, October 18, 2010: (St. Luke)

At St. John the Evangelist after Communion I could see many race cars traveling in a clockwise direction instead of counterclockwise as normal. Jesus said: *"My people, in this world of sin, a soul has to be discerning of the proper behavior to follow. If many of your friends are having pre-marital sex, it does not make it right by My law. If many of your friends are taking drugs or getting drunk, it also does not make it right by My Commandments. Just because you want to have people accept you, you do not have to follow their sinful behavior. This is how some people get attached to the wrong crowd which can lead them into trouble in their spiritual and physical lives. Even some parents can mislead their children into sex before marriage, drinking, drugs, and swearing. Every soul is given a conscience and certain behaviors have a wrong feeling that is your first warning of sinful behavior. This is why it is important for each soul to have a properly formed conscience to know right from wrong without any rationalizations. Do not just think because some friends are doing sinful behavior that it is permissible against My laws. Every soul has to stand in judgment before Me, and performing sins against Me because you thought everyone was doing it, will not make it right. You will still have to make reparation for your sinful behavior. So it is important to properly discern any of your actions by seeking My approval. Test yourself before you act. You have many temptations to commit sin every day, and one of the devil's favorite traps is that everyone is doing it. But it is not right to follow sinful behavior for any reason."*

Later, at St. Theodore's tabernacle I could see a calm picnic scene with a family next to a river on a sunny day. Then suddenly a flood appeared with a great wind that drew a man into the water. Jesus said: *"My people, in normal weather the weather people have plenty of time to forecast bad weather coming, in order to warn people to get under cover. It is when the HAARP microwave machine is used that you can see very quick violent weather appear all at once. In these cases as with tornadoes and hurricanes, the winds can change direction rapidly and put many people at risk. When bad weather persists or gets very violent, it is most likely when the HAARP machine is being used. Russia also has several of these machines and they could be enhancing storms in the Pacific Ocean. These machines can be used to cause various natural disasters which can be used against the one world people's enemies, or for causing emergencies to justify martial law. Pray for My protection from these evil ones in all of their evil plans."*

Tuesday, October 19, 2010:
(St. Issac Jogues & St. John de Brebeuf)
At St. John the Evangelist after Communion I could see how quickly expensive weapons for war could be destroyed by cheap road bombs. Jesus said: *"My people, many billions of taxpayer dollars are being spent every year on weapons and service pay for running constant wars as in Afghanistan and Iraq. The only ones benefitting from this money are the arms builders and the one world people who profit from these sales. These weapons quickly become old, and they need servicing in harsh environments. There is truly no need for constant wars for the rich to grow richer at the taxpayer expense. These wars are made up from the beginning, and peace should be prayed for instead. There is too much fraud and corruption going on in your big government programs, especially in the Defense and Security Departments. Both parties try to solve all of your problems by spending more money on*

unnecessary solutions without balancing the budgets to what taxes are collected. Without some control over your spending, your government could be bankrupted by your inept leaders."

Later, at St. Theodore's Adoration I could see how various animals, spiders, and men set traps for their victims. Jesus said: *"My people, you are familiar with how spiders make webs to trap insects for eating them. You also see how carnivorous animals lay traps to kill their prey. Man also lays traps to catch animals either for food or furs. In the spiritual world every soul has to deal with the snares and temptations of the devil. The devil has angelic powers of cunning that are beyond your powers, but your guardian angel is present to help you, if you take your angel's advice. Obvious temptations may be easier to ignore, but subtle temptations that have some good, can be more deceptive to cause sin. The devil's easier ways to get you to sin are through your weak habits. Sins that you commit often are harder to stop. Be on the alert for how the devil tries to lead you into habitual sin. Avoid places or things that lead you to sin. By being prepared in recognizing your weaknesses, you will be stronger in resisting the devil's temptations. Call on My help, your angel, and the saints to help you in avoiding sin. By prayer and frequent reception of My sacraments, you can better fend off your daily temptations from the devil."*

Wednesday, October 20, 2010:

At Holy Name after Communion I could see a huge crank and pulley that pulled the miners up out of a mine in Chile. Jesus said: *"My people, you remember vividly how desperate the people in Chile were to get the miners up from an explosion in a mine that was several thousand feet into the earth. It was a huge responsibility to drill a hole in the rock in order to get to the miners. It took several drilled holes to find them and get them out. Others had to get communications, air, and whatever else that could be sent down to them for over sixty days. The point I am making for everyone is that the more responsibility that you are given, the more will be expected of you. This is true both in your physical life, and in your spiritual life. You may be the head of the household, and your family is depending on you to hold a job and support them by providing food, clothing, and a shelter. You may also be the prayer warrior of the family and others in the family are looking up to you for spiritual guidance, and helping them save their souls. By encourag-*

ing them in Sunday Mass attendance, monthly Confession, wearing a scapular, and praying a daily rosary, you can do what you can to bring them to heaven. It is not easy to carry such heavy burdens of responsibility to save souls, but those, who have been given talents and a gift of faith, need to fulfill their missions with My help. Have trust in Me, and My faithful remnant can help many souls to avoid hell and come to heaven to receive My reward."

Later, at St. Theodore's Adoration I could see the barrels of rifles aimed at American leaders by Arab terrorists. Jesus said: *"My people, for many months American tactics in Afghanistan have used drone reaper aircraft to seek out terrorist leaders and send missiles to kill them. This has occurred even into Pakistan safe caves. These tactics have infuriated Pakistan officials and the Arab terrorists. As a reprisal, there are plans to send assassins to whatever country they can in order to attack American leaders. Your security people should be prepared for these reprisals against your leaders, especially in foreign lands. When these attacks start, there will be many attacks going on simultaneously to use the element of surprise. These terrorists have been under siege from your missile attacks, so it is understandable why they are striking back at your leaders. Pray for the safety of your leaders, but all these things are done in war. Pray also that peace could come to stop these open ended conflicts."*

Thursday, October 21, 2010:

At Holy Name after Communion I could see people debating each other over their spiritual beliefs. Jesus said: *"My people, in today's Gospel I was telling the people that some of them would believe My message of love, but others would reject My words. I am all loving, and I love everyone, both the good and the bad. What was difficult for My listeners is when I asked them to love their enemies, and to share what they had with those who are poor or in need. I even encouraged My faithful to evangelize souls to save them from hell. Many have trouble with loving their enemies, forgiving those who harmed them, and sharing their means with others. It is those people who are against My words that will give My faithful resistance and could divide people. The devil also enhances any division by planting false teachers among My faithful to try and confuse the message of My faithful. Avoid those, who teach New Age or a false faith, and cleanse them from your members.*

If you can evangelize unbelievers, then accept them, but if they refuse to believe, then they are better to be left out of your faith community. Those, who love Me, are in My sheepfold, but those, who do not believe, will be scattered."

Later, at the Eternal Father prayer group at Holy Name Adoration I could see various people losing their jobs when they even slightly said anything negative against a politically correct group. Jesus said: *"My people, there are only a few in control of your media on TV, radio, and in your newspapers. Your media is so censored and controlled because the owners can dictate what is said, or else your job is removed. You have an artificial political correctness that favors only a select number of liberal groups. Any negative comments on other groups, as Christians, does not seem to matter. As you see more persecution of Christians coming, this group will be singled out for attack as Hitler treated the Jews. Your freedoms will be diminishing as you are picked for persecution."*

I could see certain politicians employing 'dirty tricks' in their exploitation of fraudulent politics. Jesus said: *"My people, many of the current Democratic office holders have been upset by the latest 'tea party' opposition to their politics. They cannot score points with a truthful debate, so they have resorted to dirty politics by creating scenes that are trumped up to make their opposition look bad. They infiltrate organizations with radicals to make the tea party groups appear in a bad light. The people can see through these dirty tricks, and they are supporting those in favor of reduced spending. This election year will be a turning point if America can be put back on the right track. Pray for the morally correct candidates to be elected."*

I could sense a cry of injustice as many banks and corporations are reporting obscene profits. Jesus said: *"My people, because of your low bank rates on deposits and the bank bailouts from the taxpayer, many banks are making record profits, while foreclosures continue and people are losing their homes. The banks are making big money at others' expense. Your large corporations, after laying off thousands of workers, are also making huge profits from shipping jobs out of the country. The rich are getting richer, but the man in the street has less income and is getting poorer each year. This injustice will be repudiated when I return to cast the evil rich people into hell. Endure your trials for awhile until I can bring you into My Era of Peace."*

I could see some people use occult and New Age means to gain money, power, and fame in our society. Jesus said: *"My people, there are evil forces at work in your evil secret societies that are controlling all the governments of the world. Satan is directing the leaders of these one world groups because they worship Satan. This is why you are dealing with so much evil in your society starting with your many abortions. They direct your death culture, and they control your money sources. They direct what laws will be passed to continue their control. Do not judge these evil ones because My justice will come to them in the end."*

I could see the Church Year coming to a close in another month or so. Jesus said: *"My people, in the last Sundays after Pentecost you will see more readings of the end times that describe the coming Antichrist in the tribulation. Many Protestant groups talk of the end times in the Book of Revelation, but only a few priests are brave enough to talk about the end times. These end time readings are the preparations for the coming tribulation which I have given you in My messages. They are real and present to you as you see the signs all around you. You can have some Bible Study on the end time preparations so you will be ready to leave for My refuges of protection."*

In the coming days some are preparing Halloween decorations and some prefer to celebrate All Saints Day. Jesus said: *"My people, every year you see many ugly Halloween costumes and trick or treat parties that seem to encourage witches and goblins. These are almost like evil rituals, but they use children and candy treats to make it sound appealing. Sharing some candy is one thing, but you do not have to encourage any evil influences. It is better to focus on All Saints' Day than to honor an evil feast day."*

I could see people getting their books of remembrance ready for November as we celebrate the lives of those who have died during the year. Jesus said: *"My people, every year in November you give proper respect to all of those who have died during the year. You have All Saints' Day to honor those who have passed to heaven, and All Souls' Day for those who may still be suffering in purgatory. When people die, do not assume that every soul goes directly to heaven. For the most part many souls require some purification in purgatory before they can come to heaven. This is another reminder to pray for any of your family members who still may need your prayers to get out of purgatory. Having Masses said for the deceased will help them the most. Also pray for the souls who do not have anyone to pray for them."*

Saturday, October 23, 2010: (St. John of Capistrano)

At St. Patrick's Church, Kansas City, Missouri after Communion I could see the end of a large tree that had been cut down, and then there was a beautiful landscape view of some hills, mountains, and a valley. Jesus said: *"My people, as you came into church, you could see the lines for Confession before Mass. Today's Gospel also speaks of repenting for your sins. You know that I came as a man to die on a cross as a blood sacrifice for all the sins of mankind. Every Mass is an unbloody re-enactment of My sacrifice because you receive My Body and Blood at Communion time. It is important that whenever you receive Me in My Eucharist that you receive Me in the state of grace so you do not commit any sin of sacrilege against My Blessed Sacrament. To keep your soul clean in order to receive Me worthily, you should have your sins cleansed in Confession at least once every month. When the priest gives you absolution, your sins will be forgiven and My grace will be restored to your soul. Even before you enter the confessional, you should make a good examination of your conscience so you can recollect any sins that*

you have committed since your last Confession. When you come out of the confessional, remember to pray your penance and any other prayers of thanksgiving. By staying close to Me in Confession and receiving My Blessed Sacrament often, then you will be strengthened to endure your daily temptations of the devil, and help evangelize souls for heaven. When you see so much evil in the world, you need to strive to save as many souls as you can from hell with My help."

Sunday, October 24, 2010:

At St. Anthony's Church, Camdenton, Missouri after Communion I could see a cornucopia of graces pouring out on all of God's people. Jesus

said: *"My people, My love for all of you is overflowing as My graces are poured out on you from this vision of the cornucopia, or some call it a horn of plenty. Even when you come to Me in prayer, I am always ready to answer your prayer. I have said: 'Ask and you will receive, knock and the door will be opened for you.' In the Gospel parable it is better to come to Me as the tax collector who came humbly into My presence. All the saints felt that they were unworthy in coming to Me. The Pharisee was commendable in what he did, but by bragging and belittling others, he offended Me with his self righteousness. In the end those who exalt themselves will be humbled, while those who humble themselves will be exalted. When you come to Me in prayer, have trust that I will hear and answer your prayer in what is best for your soul and the souls who you are praying for. Give praise and thanksgiving to Me for all the physical gifts that I send to you, and all the graces that I give you for your spiritual protection."*

Monday, October 25, 2010:

At the Ascension Church Adoration Chapel, Overland Park, Kansas I could see a modern church and a religion class being taught their lesson. Jesus said: *"My people, there is a battle of good and evil going on all around you every day where both sides are fighting for souls. You may find yourself in some churches where they teach New Age principles, and they belittle My Blessed Mother's rosary. Beware when anyone teaches heretical facts against the faith. If someone teaches that Bible stories are myths, if they teach New Age worship and Reiki, or they teach that sexual sins are no longer sins, then you need to stand up and witness against such teachings. You may get persecuted and put down because some clergy think that they are more intelligent than you are. My laity will save My Church from such clergy that teach heresies. If you cannot change this heretical teaching, then move to a church that teaches correctly. This is another sign that the division is coming soon in My Church where the schismatic church will be separated from My faithful remnant. You eventually will be forced to have Masses in the home if you can find a faithful priest. The persecution of Christians will get so bad with some being martyred that you will then have to call on Me and your guardian angel to lead you to My refuges of protection. When you are confronted by heretical teaching in the religion classes, you also should speak out against such errors. Even if they throw you out of such classes, at least you have warned the people of false teaching. Do not let those teaching heresies go unchallenged when you know they are teaching against My Church laws and My Commandments. You will be rewarded in heaven for defending the faith. But those who do nothing against heresies could suffer in purgatory for condoning such lies by their inaction. Pray for My discernment in all that you hear from the pulpit and in person, and let the Holy Spirit speak through you to answer such heresies."*

Later, at the Ascension Church, Overland Park, Kansas after Communion I could see someone who was tormented by a demon. Jesus said: *"My people, in the Gospel I healed a woman of a demon who had been torturing her for eighteen years, and still I received criticism for healing her on the Sabbath.*(Luke 13:10-17) *Demons even today are torturing people with various addictions from drinking, drugs, gambling, computers, smoking, and overeating. People have various weaknesses to sin and some of these tendencies are inherited. Most all of these excessive addictions are associated with demons. In order to heal these addictions, the first step is to admit that you have a problem, and the second step is to desire to heal your addiction. In all cases you need to pray for a healing, and have faith in Me that you can be healed. If you cannot heal your addiction on your own, then you may need counseling or a withdrawal from what is causing the addiction. Prayers, healing from healers, exorcisms, or miracles can also help in healing addictions. The price of removing an addiction could be high and it could require persistent prayer and fasting over some years. Even Mass intentions could help remove the demons. By realizing that demons are attached to addictions, then you can see that this is a spiritual battle to win with My help. Never give up on any healing, and be persistent in your prayers for any person with an addiction."*

Tuesday, October 26, 2010:

At St. John the Evangelist after Communion I could see a man and wife after they got married. Jesus said: *"My people, in St. Paul's day the husband had more authority as the head of the household, which is why in the first reading he asked the wives to be subordinate to their husbands. He also said that husbands should love their wives as I love My Church. The family is the unit of the fabric of your society, but there are many attacks on the family from divorce, living together, and unnatural marriages that have split families. Now only a third of households are husband and wife. When your society breaks down in its morality, your country is also headed to ruin as well. Abortion and birth control are further signs of a disrespect for life and the poor care of children. Your society is more focused on lust, pleasure, and comforts. This is why sin is rampant in your society, which will bring your destruction. The family needs to be supported as an ideal for living instead of a tradition that some want to discard as old fashioned. America was great when it recognized Me in your documents, but now that you are turning your back on Me, your greatness will fall."*

Later, at Holy Name after Communion I could see a tower like the Leaning Tower of Pisa, but this represented the fall of America. Jesus said: *"My people, I showed you a leaning tower and all the dimensions and forces that were necessary to cause the tower to fall. At a certain angle, gravity would cause the tower to accelerate toward its fall. America, with its internal moral decay, is already reaching past the point of no return. This means that the evil you see today, is accelerating at an ever increasing rate until you will enter the evil of the Antichrist's tribulation. Do not give up hope because evil will grow worse before I come to vanquish all the evil ones. Instead, call on My grace of protection by help from My angels, and they will lead you to My refuges. My refuges will be your safe havens from those who will be trying to kill you. Some will be martyred for their faith, while the rest of My faithful remnant will be safe at My refuges. Do not worry, but have trust in Me, even when the persecution will get much worse than now. Evil will have a short reign before I will intervene and cast this evil lot into hell. I will then renew the earth and bring My faithful into My Era of Peace."*

Wednesday, October 27, 2010:

At Holy Name after Communion I could see a dark cave for protection, but a light will be needed. Jesus said: *"My people, whenever you see a dark cave as in the vision, there is always some uncertainty as to whether there are animals present or not. When you are led to caves for protection, you will need your windup flashlights to see into the darkness. Your angels will protect you even from any threatening animals in the caves. Caves can be cold and moist, so it would be a good idea to set up your tents in the caves for warmth and some protection from any moist ground. You may need to stay closer to the opening for air to breathe and some daylight. There is also spiritual darkness in life that also needs My Light of grace to take away any fear of the evil around you. Trust in My leading you through the trials of this life on earth. Without Me you can do nothing, but with My help you will have direction and purpose to your mission in life. At times you are tested in your faith, but by trusting in Me, you will find the right path to My Kingdom in the Gospel reading, where I will open the door to My faithful."*

For Carl: Jesus said: *"Marion sends you her love* (to Carl) *because you need some comforting in her passing. She will be in purgatory a short time as the Masses will bring her to heaven. She will be watching over Carl and praying for his help in this time of mourning. He can call on her as an intercessor for prayer requests. I see her looking down on her old home on Shale Drive. She was very happy to have John and Carol as neighbors for so long, and she thanks the two of you for your love and your friendship."*

Later, at St. Theodore's Adoration I could see a crane representing how the Democrats have changed America. Jesus said: *"My people, this election will be a chance for voters to vote against all of your president's socialist agenda. His 'change' has given you a health plan that will eventually demand computer chips in the body. He has helped close many banks under the FDIC. Many large banks were bailed out, and many toxic assets are a taxpayer liability with the takeover of Freddie Mac and Fannie Mae. Two car companies were taken over and many large deficits were put in place with little accounting for how the money was spent. The high unemployment rate is still a result of the one world people's plan to eliminate all manufacturing in America. This has been carried out by your large corporations who have exported many jobs to China, India, and other third world countries. If this trend is not stopped, America will have only the rich and the poor with no jobs for the middle class. Without good incomes, there will be less taxes to support your growing welfare state that will collapse under its own weight of debts. Your finances are close to bankruptcy, even if your Federal Reserve buys more worthless Treasury Notes. The dollar is artificially controlled, and its true value is rapidly decreasing as measured against commodities and other currencies. Once your bankruptcy is completed, then you will see your takeover into the North American Union. Martial law will be declared and I will warn My faithful when it is time to leave for My refuges to avoid being killed by the one world armies. Be prepared for the coming tribulation both spiritually and physically. Once you see the Antichrist come to power, then you know that My coming is near when I will defeat these evil ones."*

Thursday, October 28, 2010: (St. Simon & St. Jude)
At Holy Name after Communion I could see a small hole at first and then the hole grew deeper and deeper into the size of a water well. Jesus said: *"My people, this hole in the vision that grew deeper and deeper, refers to America's problems both physically and spiritually. You are digging a deeper hole in financial debts with your rapidly expanding deficits which are also challenging the value of your dollar currency. A deeper hole in debt threatens not only your current standard of living, but it even threatens the future of your children who will be paying the interest on the higher National Debt. If these debts get much worse, there is a chance of bankruptcy of America, and a disruption of your whole money system. Spiritually, you are also digging a deeper hole where your sins are outweighing the prayers and good works being done by your people. Corruption in your government and business world has been driven by greed and the desire for power by the one world people to take over your country and turn you into their slaves. My justice will be bringing My punishment upon your nation, just as Israel was exiled for worshiping other gods. Unless your people repent and change their lives for the better, America will bring its own ruin upon itself."*

Later, at the Eternal Father prayer group at the Holy Name Adoration I could see the altar filled with beautiful late flowers. Jesus said: *"My people, many of your flowers and vegetables have had an even longer growing season without having a frost. The changing leaves and mums are still adding color to your landscape before winter descends on you. When you have the bright sunshine on your changing leaves, the colors are bright and vivid as well. You have captured some fall beauty in your pictures. Thank you for those who dress the altar to give Me glory from the beauty of My creation."*

I could see the candidates giving their last minute push to get elected. Jesus said: *"My people, some will be happy when all the signs and ads stop after your coming election is over. Some have been encouraging the voters to change the current socialist government that is being forced on you from the current administration. Some politicians predict a change in the seats of your Congress, but the vote still has to be counted. Every election year is an opportunity to change your country's direction to a better position on the moral laws of your government. Your abortion laws need to stop abortions, and your death culture needs to be changed. Pray for the candidates who are morally right to lead your country. Your people need to do their civil responsibility to get out and vote for the right candidates."*

I could see America leaning more to the left in many of the bills being passed. Jesus said: *"My people, if your voters do not stand up to the current left leaning Congress, then socialism will take away your remaining rights. Fight for your Constitutional rights, or you could even see your sovereignty rights taken away when you could be forced to accept the North American Union. Vote for those candidates who will rein in your deficit spending so your budget could become balanced."*

I could see very negative ads that are trying to put down the 'Tea Party'. Jesus said: *"My people, the Congress people in office are afraid to run on their voting record when it is exposed, which is why they do not want to debate the true issues. Instead, they have focused on negative ads in great quantity hoping to put the 'Tea Party' opposition in any bad light they can. They even produce false stories in their favor because the media is very liberal in its portrayal of news events. See through these made up stories and the censored news that you have to tolerate every day."*

I could see a tide of evil flowing over America because of our corrupt politicians. Jesus said: *"My people, because of your media blackout on the important issues of your government, you are not finding out how corrupt and even ruthless your Congress is in forcing legislation on you that is not even read or examined. These bills being pushed through are against your freedoms, and that is why these corrupt politicians do not want you to know what is said in the hidden lines of their bills. Pray again for your voters to root out this leftist corruption that is stealing away your Constitutional rights."*

I could see the coming celebration of All Saints' Day and All Souls' Day. Jesus said: *"My people, All Souls' Day should be a day of obligation for all Catholics to come to Mass. The less you abide by My Church laws on days of obligation, the harder it will be to have My faithful follow other Church laws. There are only a handful of such Holy days celebrated for the whole year. It is also fitting that you honor all the saints who have struggled through trials and sufferings to gain their crowns in heaven. Pray for the souls in purgatory and pray to My saints as intercessors for your petitions."*

I could see people raking and bagging their leaves as they fall from the trees. Jesus said: *"My people, as the leaves fall from your trees, they are littered all over your lawn which makes it look untidy. When you rake up the leaves, your lawn looks cleansed just as when you come to Confession and your sins are cleansed from your souls. Even at times you may feel like you are evangelizing souls as you rake your leaves and bag them. Reach out to all souls so you can help them to avoid going to hell. You would much rather see souls being taken up to heaven than burning in the flames of hell."*

Friday, October 29, 2010: (Bishop Clark's Mass for the 43rd Anniversary of Holy Name) At Holy Name after Communion I could see a gold aura around the monstrance of Adoration on the altar of our church. Jesus said: *"My people, the people of this church have been blessed by My Presence for forty-three years as you are seeing My Blessed Sacrament exposed on the altar in the vision. All of My churches have been under attack to be closed. The churches that are still surviving, are a tribute to the parishioners and the pastors of those churches. You have been blessed by a strong pastor who is working hard to keep your church open. Give thanks and praise to Me because My sacramental Presence is what makes your churches holy. It is difficult to suffer the closing of many churches, but it is a sign of how lukewarm many Catholics have become in their faith. Once people stop coming to Sunday Mass, then your faith community is weakened by that loss. Pray for your church members to be strong in their faith, and that they will work to support your church and your pastor in all that is needed to keep your church open. This is one more battle that you face in the temptations of spiritual laziness. Pray that your people will keep strong in their prayer life, and receive My sacraments often."*

Later, at St. Theodore's tabernacle I could see a large fish about to eat some smaller fish. Jesus said: *"My people, there are predators looking to make money on people in all walks of life. You have seen many scams on Wall Street that have stolen people's life savings. These evil people have greed and a desire for power in their hearts and souls. Many kinds of fraud are usually found out and captured, but some get away with their theft. I see all of their evil deeds and they will have to stand before Me in judgment. The difficulty is how do My people deal with such evil-minded people. There are various ways to steal people's identity, and everyone is vulnerable to such attacks. The best that you can do is to make it harder for evil ones to access your information. In the end you have to deal with any losses, but losing money is not the end of your life. Money and possessions can be replaced to some extent, but it is your soul that is more important to guard. This is why you still have to love everyone despite their imperfections. Do not let such losses affect your love relationships, but try to reconcile any problems and move on with the rest of your life."*

Saturday, October 30, 2010:

At St. John the Evangelist after Communion I could see a crown of thorns hanging over a cross. Jesus said: *"My people, this crown of thorns over My cross represents how My Blessed Mother shared all of My sufferings as I died on the cross. It is very difficult to see your son so brutally crucified, even when I committed no crime. But My Blessed Mother knew that I had to suffer as a price for the salvation of all of mankind's sins. This is why My Blessed Mother can console anyone who has suffered the loss of a loved one. Pray to My Blessed Mother as an intercessor for your petitions because I listen closely to her requests. Wherever you see Me, My Blessed Mother is with Me because our two hearts are always united. My Blessed Mother watches over her children as she loves Me, so let her mantle of protection be always at your side. When you pray your rosaries for her intentions, she will always have My ear to hear them."*

Later, at St. Cecilia's tabernacle I could see some Franciscans, Redemptorists, and Jesuits as missionaries. Jesus said: *"My people, there are various orders of priests and brothers who are called to be missionaries and help convert souls to the faith. Some Franciscans pray and work in monasteries. Some Redemptorists give missions or retreats for the people. Some Jesuits go to other foreign countries to win souls to the faith. I even send various messengers out to share My Gospel of love, but also some to prepare refuges for the coming tribulation. I told you before as the time of tribulation grows close, that many messengers will be receiving more messages about refuge preparation. As the persecution of Christians will grow worse, My faithful will need My refuges for*

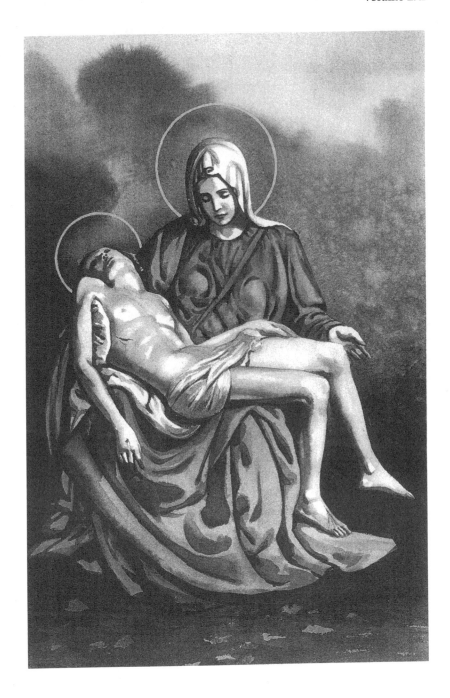

physical and spiritual protection. I call all of My faithful in addition to those mentioned to go out and evangelize souls to the faith. Some will be converted for the first time, while the lukewarm need to be reconverted."

Sunday, October 31, 2010:
At Holy Name after Communion I could see a Bible open to today's reading from St. Paul. Jesus said: "*My people, when people speak of the end times, they think of it as a long time off beyond their lifetime without any concern. It is true that I have told you to carry on with your mission and not just to stop and wait for the end to come. I have also told you not to have fear of the end times, and to trust in My protection. On the other hand, I have reminded you several times that these events will happen in your lifetime, so you need to be prepared for what to do. You need to be like the five wise virgins who had extra oil for their lamps, and they were prepared for the Wedding Banquet. Since you do not know if I will come tomorrow, you need to have your soul ready to meet Me at the judgment on any day by frequent Confession, at least monthly. Your mission is also to warn people to have their backpacks, blankets, and tents ready now for when you will need to leave for My refuges. It will be at My refuges that you will be protected by My angels from the evil ones who will be trying to kill you. These refuges will be at My Blessed Mother's places of apparition, places of holy ground, monasteries, and caves. When I warn you that it is time to go, call on Me and I will have your guardian angels lead you to the nearest refuge with a physical flame. You will have to leave quickly, preferably at night. Be thankful that I will be protecting you, and that you have been given information on what to take, and how you will be living away from your homes in safety. So do not take the end times lightly because with your eyes of faith, you are seeing all the signs now that are leading up to the Antichrist's takeover.*"

Monday, November 1, 2010: (All Saints' Day)
At Holy Name after Communion I could see St. Therese come in her brown clothing. St. Therese said: "*My son, I am happy to guide you in your work for My Jesus. Do not be upset at any of your unintended mistakes in judgment. Make amends with anyone that you may have indirectly harmed and move on with your work and prayer. Do not let*

the devil use these impediments to discourage you from your work in any way. In considering doing another DVD, you know the attacks that you received in your previous DVD. You know my Novena for help, so call on my prayer as an intercessor to protect you from any spiritual harassment in this effort. The more you pray at the beginning of your work, the easier it will go for you. Keep me in mind in your prayers and I will be watching out for you and protecting you."

Later, at St. Theodore's tabernacle I could see a train carrying passengers that were dressed as if they lived in the 1920's. Jesus said: *"My people, there are two ways that the one world people could pull off a takeover without using viruses to kill a lot of people. One way would be to turn off the electric grid which would stop gasoline pumps, some factories, many communications, water pumps, refrigerators, banks, computers, televisions, and regular lighting. No electricity would cause people to live a much simpler life with little travel. Another means that could send your technology back to the 1920s is an EMP* (Electromagnetic Pulse) *attack either from bombs or EMP weapons. This attack would stop your vehicles from moving and it would destroy all of your microchips that run computers and many of your appliances. If the electricity was turned off, it could be restored at any time by the one world people who want to take over. If an EMP attack was used, computers and chips would have to be stored deep underground so they could restart a society later under the one world control. In either case, My faithful could seek My refuges for food and shelter without any need of electricity or chips in order to survive. You have become dependent on many electrical comforts that you will have taken away from you when it is time to go to My refuges. Be prepared to live a much more rustic life with a lot less comforts than you have today."*

Tuesday, November 2, 2010: (All Souls' Day)

At Holy Name after Communion I could see the souls in purgatory suffering in the flames. Jesus said: *"My people, you know of My mercy in saving souls from hell, but you also know of My justice where only pure souls can enter into heaven. As your priests mentioned, there is My forgiveness of repentant sinners, but there also is reparation for those sins that need to be satisfied in some way as well. Some do their reparation or suffering on earth to save them time in purgatory. Others need to be purified in purgatory. Even in purgatory there are two general sufferings. The lower parts of purgatory suffer from the burning flames as in hell, and they cannot be in My presence, but they are promised one day to enter heaven. These souls are spirits only, and they can sometimes communicate with the people on earth. The upper parts of purgatory are not suffering the flames, but they are in a grey, dingy area, and they also cannot be in My presence. These souls see each other, but they cannot comfort each other. Time in purgatory is no longer relevant because these souls are outside of time, and their suffering seems longer. Once you have a sense of how much these souls suffer, then you want to help alleviate their time there. My faithful can pray for these souls to lessen their time, and Masses said for them are an even greater help. Some souls have to suffer a minimum time in purgatory before your prayers can benefit them. So in your daily prayers, do not forget to pray for the release of souls in purgatory, especially those in your own family who may still be suffering there."*

Later, at St. Theodore's tabernacle I could see a tunnel to an underground city to protect the one world people. Jesus said: *"My people, you have heard and have been given messages about many underground cities that were built to protect the one world people. One message, that has been given a lot of press, is about a massive corona discharge that could kill a lot of people with particles from the sun. While this is possible, your research has shown it to be improbable. Protection underground could more likely be needed if there were riots over food shortages, massive EMP attacks that would set off a martial law, or a very deadly virus attack that would reduce the population. Just as the one world people will seek these underground cities, so My faithful will need My protection at My refuges. There, I will shield you from the one world armies, bombs, EMP attacks, virus attacks, or attacks from the sun. Whatever means that the evil ones will use for a takeover, My angels will protect My faithful at My refuges. So have no fear of the evil ones as I will be guarding your bodies and your souls."*

Wednesday, November 3, 2010: (St. Martin de Porres)

At Holy Name after Communion I could see deer meat being cooked on a spit at a refuge. Jesus said: *"My people, I have told you at My refuges how I will provide the food for you by allowing deer to drop dead in your camps, as in the Exodus when the quail dropped dead in their camps. It will be the responsibility of your community to bleed and hang the deer, as well as using your deer knives to cut them up. Once prepared, then you are seeing deer parts roasted on a fire with a turning spit in the vision. You will have shelters and food provided, but you will need to clean, make beds, wash clothes, and prepare food as in past days without your modern appliances. This rustic living will keep you more focused on Me in prayer while you are protected from the evil ones. Give Me thanks and praise for how I take care of your needs even now."*

Later, at St. Theodore's Adoration I could see a deep cave where scientists were experimenting on making deadly viruses for reducing the population. Jesus said: *"My people, I have warned you that the one world people have been secretly producing one virus scare after another. The most recent H1N1 virus of Swine Flu was designed to be highly contagious, but it was not very deadly. The interesting part is that the one world people wanted everyone to take their Swine Flu shot and the seasonal flu shot together. I have encouraged My faithful to avoid taking any flu shots because this will be the method to make everyone susceptible to the deadly pandemic virus that they plan to release by the chemtrails. You have seen on TV programs and on the internet how there are hundreds of secret germ labs all over your country. It is a fact that AIDS and other viruses were made and released for the purpose of reducing the population. This is part of the death culture led by Satan. I will warn My faithful to go to My refuges before this pandemic virus will be released. By looking on the luminous cross and drinking the healing spring water, My people will be healed of any viruses that the evil ones are working on. Have no fear of these deadly viruses because I will shield you from them, but the evil people will reduce the population to some extent according to their evil plan. Trust in Me that I will cast all of these evil ones into hell, while I will prepare My Era of Peace for My followers."*

Thursday, November 4, 2010: (St. Charles Borromeo)
At Holy Name after Communion I could see an entrance and there was a rainbow all around the entrance. Jesus said: *"My people, in today's Gospel I gave two parables about finding a lost sheep and a lost coin to emphasize how heaven rejoices over every repentant sinner. In order to repent, souls have to make an act of their free will to be sorry for their sins and seek My forgiveness. I want everyone to love Me, but I do not*

41

force Myself on you. It is your free will to love Me or not, but when love is shown freely, this is cause for celebration. The rainbow in the Old Testament was My covenant with man that I would never destroy life on earth with a flood ever again. It is this covenant that I am emphasizing in the vision when I died for your sins on the cross. For those, who repent of their sins and follow My Commandments, I will offer them eternal life in heaven. There may be some purification needed on earth or in purgatory, but I will keep My promise of My reward in heaven for My faithful. When souls enter heaven, there is even more rejoicing when they receive their crowns of glory in My eternal presence."

Later, at the Eternal Father prayer group at Holy Name Adoration I could see a vision of the Statue of Liberty. Jesus said: *"My people, your elections have sent a strong message to the Democrats that the people are against them for taking their freedoms away, and for their socialist policies that have enabled government to grow more into everyone's lives. The largest requests were for less spending, reduced deficits, and help with getting jobs for people. Some parts of your society were against the Health Law that will raise costs more than lower them. Some want various health insurance coverages, but no one wants to pay for them. Now that the elections are over, it will be a challenge for all those who were elected to make some hard choices."*

I could see people being forced to have National ID cards for health insurance, and then they were forced to take chips in the body. Jesus said: *"My people, you saw in the original Health Bill a place indicating that chips in the body would be required for insurance benefits. This is the ultimate plan of the one world people to force mandatory chips in the body on everyone. These officials will mandate a National ID with a smart chip in it. This will be the first stage, and then chips in the body will be demanded so you do not lose your chip identification. Remember to place aluminum foil over all chipped documents to protect against identity theft and prevent tracking. Refuse to take any chips in your body because they will control your mind. When this comes, leave for My refuges."*

I could see the value of the dollar going down with the latest Federal Reserve buying of Treasury Notes. Jesus said: *"My people, this 'Quantitative Easing' of your Federal Reserve to buy $900 billion worth of Treasury Notes is a disguise to purposely lower the value of the dollar in the name of boosting the economy. They already have bought $1.8 trillion worth of Treasury Notes the first time, and this did not help that much. This is purposely increasing the National Debt with no promise that it will stimulate the economy. This action places America one step closer to bankruptcy which is the real plan for a martial law takeover. Many of these massive spending plans were never voted by the people, but they were forced on you by the one world people. Stimulus spending and bank bailouts have helped only the rich, but they are mortgaging your children's future. Pray that the deficit spending, stimulus spending, and other useless spending could be brought under control before America becomes bankrupt."*

I could see the Washington Monument that stands 666 feet tall from its base underground as a Masonic symbol of control in full view. Jesus said: *"My people, there is considerable Masonic influence behind the scenes that is controlling your government, even from the roots of the Masonic symbols in Washington, D.C.'s design. It is not by accident that most all the Cabinet posts are given to one world controlled people who belong to the Council on Foreign Relations, the Bilderbergs, and the Trilateral Commission. This is why neither party will change the one world people's plans because their people are always in control with puppets leading your country. Pray for true freedom through your representatives, and not just the following of orders from the one world people and Satan."*

I could see newscasters talking about more plans to expand NAFTA. Jesus said: *"My people, the one world people brought about the European Union with no votes from the people. Now, your recent Presidents have supported and expanded your North American Free Trade Agreement (NAFTA). This is the path to forming the North American Union that combines America, Mexico, and Canada. This plan will take away your sovereignty rights and let these one world people make you into their slaves. Fight against this union that will put you closer into the Antichrist's power. Once this union is formed, you will need to leave for My refuges."*

I could see many expensive new weapons being made for the military. Jesus said: *"My people, you are aware that your government's largest budget item is for your Defense Department which pays for your military people and their weapons and bases. Here again the one world people cause constant wars so your military people are never home to defend their own people, and your deficits are increased. This is one more means of worthless spending to bankrupt your country. Wars never have winners, but the rich prosper on the weapons' sales. Pray for peace and more control by the people over any choices for war."*

I could see how many 'Tea Party' people are putting the Republicans on probation for returning to their conservative roots with less wars. Jesus said: *"My people, on the surface it appears that the Republicans have taken back many seats that were lost because the people were tired of your previous President's wars and deficits. Now the new 'Tea Party' faction wants Republicans to turn back to their principles against deficits and a return of their lost freedoms. Without a serious change in their policies, there may even be another formation of a third party. Pray for more reasonable spending, and policies that are for the people and not for the ruling one world people."*

Friday, November 5, 2010:

At St. John the Evangelist after Communion I could see new weapons that use powerful laser beams and EMP weapons. Jesus said: *"My people, your current military weapons have some serious consequences if they are fully deployed. Some weapons can melt metal tanks, some lasers can inactivate incoming missiles, while some EMP* (Electromagnetic Pulse) *weapons could paralyze whole cities or armies that use microchips in their equipment. EMP weapons can simulate the effects of neutron bombs. Their powerful rays can destroy microchips that would stop vehicles, computers, and any appliances that use microchips. Modern armies rely on microchips to run vehicles, target the enemy tanks, and many guidance systems for missiles. If EMP weapons were used, aircraft carriers and whole armies could be neutralized. If these weapons fell into the wrong hands, America's existence could be changed back to old technology. None of these weapons could harm My faithful at My refuges, so My protection is far superior to any of man's weapons. Be aware of your military's capabilities, but remember that I have a greater power than all of these evil ones. In the end My power will triumph over the Antichrist and Satan, as My faithful will be rewarded in My Era of Peace and then into heaven."*

Later, at Holy Name Divine Mercy Holy Hour I could see a priest standing in front of the two tablets of the Ten Commandments. Jesus said: *"My people, this vision of a priest standing before the Ten Commandments, means the priest in his homilies needs to emphasize the need for frequent Confession. You are all sinners and are in need of My forgiveness. Some rationalize their mortal sins into venial sins, and think they do not have to go to Confession. Even if you only have venial sins, you should make a practice of going to at least monthly Confession. There are many preparations for Confession to examine your conscience for your past sins. Unless you come to Confession, you do not have My absolution that forgives your sins and restores grace to your souls. My priests also need to warn the people that if they have mortal sin on their souls, they should not receive Me in Holy Communion because they would be committing another mortal sin of sacrilege. My priests should also emphasize that I am truly Present in My Body and Blood in every consecrated Host, and the people need to genuflect to My tabernacle on entering and leaving My church. By confessing your sins and giving honor to My Blessed Sacrament, you will have sufficient graces to protect yourself from the devil's daily temptations."*

Saturday, November 6, 2010:

At St. John the Evangelist after Communion I could see the money changers in the Temple when Jesus turned over their tables. Jesus said: *"My people, there are many people in your society where their greed for money, power, and possessions have turned them into money worshipers instead of worshiping Me. It is bad enough to be addicted to wealth and power, but it is even worse when the rich steal money from the people in planned stock crashes, and from the taxpayers who have bailed out their losses. Your financial crisis has been purposely manufactured by the financiers of Wall Street in order to steal money from innocent investors. Now the central bankers of your Federal Reserve want to lower the value of your currency until it is worthless, so they can replace the dollar with the amero of the North American Union. I have warned My people of the rich elites that are planning a bankruptcy of America for the takeover of your country through martial law. Once they strip you of your dollar's value, then they will try to force mandatory chips in the body. When you see this collapse of America and the riots that will follow, refuse to take any chips in the body, and call on Me to lead you to the safety of My refuges."*

Sunday, November 7, 2010:

At Holy Name after Communion I could see some crowns in heaven waiting to be given to the souls in purgatory once they are purified. Jesus said: *"My people, in today's Gospel the Sadducees, who did not believe in the resurrection of the body, were trying to test Me with their story of the seven brothers who married the same woman. I told them that they were greatly mistaken, and that the souls in heaven are like angels who do not marry. Heaven is a spiritual kingdom, and the bodies of the faithful will only be joined with their souls at the last judgment. When people die in this life, only very few souls come directly to heaven. Some souls go to hell, and the rest need purification in purgatory. This is why Masses and prayers are said for the dead, so those who are in purgatory can be helped by shortening their time there. Praying for the souls in purgatory should be one of your daily prayer intentions. In the deacon's homily it should also have been mentioned how important Confession should be in protecting your soul from going to hell. By frequent repenting of your sins in Confession, you can have your souls cleansed of sin, and you will be in the state of grace and ready to receive Me at your judgment on the day of your death. One day the souls in purgatory are promised to be with Me in heaven, and then they will receive their crowns of sainthood that you saw in the vision."*

Later, at St. Joseph's place during the rosary I could see an empty chair that represented how many prayer warriors are dying off. Jesus said: *"My people, this empty chair is a sign that many of My prayer warriors are dying, and the younger generation is not as prayerful. It is important for My prayer warriors to teach their children how to pray the rosary, and to be faithful to praying it every day. You are dealing with a spiritual battle between good and evil, and the number of prayers cannot decrease, or evil will gain in the world. This is why it is necessary that for every prayer warrior that dies, you need to have other prayer warriors to take their place. Continue to ask Me to double your prayers and to have My angels finish your rosaries if you fall asleep. Also, I continue to remind you to make up any missed rosaries on the following day. I depend on the prayers of My prayer warriors to balance the evil in your world. When the prayers diminish to a certain level, Satan and the Antichrist will be allowed their hour at the time of the tribulation. This loss of faith and poor prayer lives are a sign of the end days beginning. Be prepared to come to My refuges when the tribulation begins."*

Monday, November 8, 2010:

At St. John the Evangelist after Communion I could see the printing presses putting out the daily newspaper. Jesus said: *"My people, in this vision of the daily printing of your newspaper, this reminds you of how anxious you are to read the daily news so you are kept up to date on what is happening in the world. I want to contrast this to My Good News in the Bible which keeps you up to date with what is happening in the spiritual world of your soul. You have one news for the body, and another news for the soul. But it is your soul that is everlasting, and your body is temporary and lasts but a short lifetime. So My Good News of how to live a proper spiritual life should be of more concern for your eternal life and your destination than any worldly news. Another reason, that I want you to read your Bible more, is so you can put the readings at Mass into their full context. Notice which readings are going to be read, and then read what comes before and after the reading so this can enhance your understanding of My message in the Scriptures. By quiet contemplation on these readings, you will be better trained in your faith, and better able to direct your spiritual life. I love all of you, and I want everyone to take full advantage of all that I have revealed to you in My Word. Once you see how important My Good News is over your worldly news, you can look forward more to hearing My Word that lasts forever, beyond your worldly news that is old after you read it."*

Later, at St. Theodore's tabernacle I could see some small flat black chips that were coming off of a manufacturing line, and these were the chips to be implanted in the body that could control people's minds with voices. Jesus said: *"My people, there have been many advances in your microchip manufacturing, especially for chips that could be implanted in the body. These chips in the vision were especially designed for mind control and your government has produced millions of them to go along with your latest Health Care bill. Initially, there will be smart cards as national ID cards for tracking, buying and selling, as well as for health care. The next stage planned is to make it mandatory to have a microchip in the body so the one world people could control you like robots. The authorities will not tell you that they are mind control chips, but that is what they will be using. Refuse to take any chips in the body, even if they threaten to kill you and deny you health care. This is the mark of the beast to avoid, and once they are made mandatory, then it is time to come to My refuges. At My refuges you will be healed of all of your ailments by looking on My luminous cross. My health plan is much better than that of your current President. Trust in My protection at My refuges where I will provide for all of your needs."*

Tuesday, November 9, 2010:
(Dedication of St. John Lateran Basilica)

At Holy Name after Communion I could see a wooden wheel with spokes all around and candle flames at the inside of every spoke. Jesus said: *"My people, St. John Lateran Basilica is the Cathedral of Rome, and it is where many popes resided before St. Peter's Basilica was built. On this feast day of its dedication, this church is like a hub for all the Roman Catholic churches as in the vision. You saw in the Gospel how I cast the money changers out of the Temple for making it a marketplace instead of a place of worship. St. John quoted from Psalm 68:10 'Zeal for your house consumes Me' meaning how much My churches are holy because My very Presence resides there in My tabernacles. When the Jews asked for a sign of why I threw out the money changers, I told them 'Destroy this temple* (of My body) *and in three days I will rebuild it.' This was a sign of My coming death and resurrection, but they did not understand that I was referring to the temple of My Body. This is a reminder also of how your bodies are Temples of the Holy Spirit in the same description of your body. So rejoice in coming to My churches, but I am also present in My people."*

Later, at St. Theodore's Adoration I could see the volcano in Indonesia continue to have explosive releases of smoke and ash. Jesus said: *"My people, this current volcanic release of smoke and ash has been going on for nearly a month. Even your President's visit to Indonesia had to be cut short because it is difficult to fly jet planes near such active volcanoes. Several years ago, a large 9.2 earthquake in this area triggered eleven volcanoes back to life in lava flows. Now a recent 7.7 earthquake in Indonesia has caused a less severe tsunami and has brought more volcanoes into an active state. This current volcano* (Merapi Volcano) *has caused hundreds of deaths and more people are being evacuated. The longer these eruptions spew more smoke and ash into the upper atmosphere, you have a chance to block out the sun, and it can cause a cooling effect over the earth. Also, the more active the earthquakes and volcanoes get, this could affect other areas along the fault lines of the Pacific Ring of Fire. Be prepared to witness more natural disasters, even as your hurricane season is just finishing. Pray that those being affected by the earthquakes and the volcano will find enough aid to get them through these latest disasters."*

Wednesday, November 10, 2010: (St. Leo the Great, Pope)

At St. John the Evangelist after Communion I could see two light posts where one was lit and the other was off. Jesus said: *"My people, in the Gospel there were ten lepers that I healed, but only a Samaritan returned to give thanks for his healing. I told him to go as his faith had saved him. There are also the lukewarm in the faith vs. My prayer warriors. This is the contrast in the vision where some faithful are beacons of faith and hope, but the lukewarm have their light out because of their spiritual laziness. But those, who pray and do good works in evangelizing souls, are the souls that I will welcome into heaven. The lukewarm, who only call on Me when they are in need and do not help people, may have the gates of heaven closed to them if they do not wake up. Also, My faithful need to be thanking Me for all that I do for you. Give praise and glory to your Lord, and you will have My promise of eternal life in heaven."*

Later, at St. Theodore's Adoration I could first see a waste basket, and then a scene of water in a pool. Jesus said: *"My people, when you are before Me in Adoration, you can contemplate how best to improve your spiritual life. When you see this waste basket, it reminds you of what sinful habits that you would like to discard into the basket. There are certain sins that you repeat in Confession many times. Think of your worst habitual sin, and try to focus on how you can best avoid that sin. Pray to Me to give you the grace to overcome that weakness in your life. As you see the water in the pool, think of how your sins could be cleansed from your soul, and how you could work to keep your soul pure. By working to rid your habitual sins, then you could be making progress in striving for your perfection. If you allow yourself to fall back into your old habits, then pick yourself up, and struggle back to where you have progressed before. By keeping your focus on Me, and keeping yourself strong in the face of temptations, then you can make some true progress in your spiritual life."*

Thursday, November 11, 2010: (St. Martin of Tours)

At Holy Name after Communion I could see a large black evil eye up close that represented the devil or evil ones watching me. Jesus said: *"My son, you are seeing a frightening look at the black eye of the evil one who is always trying to attack you and your ministry. Whenever you are doing good things in your prayers, good works for people, or attempts at evangelizing people, you are going to get attacks from the evil ones. Fear not, My son, for I send you angels of protection because your ministry is important to prepare My people for the coming tribulation. As you are preparing your next DVD, it is important to do your novena prayers for the success of this project. You will be attacked to put this off, so work hard on finishing this work every day. This time is crucial because the evil forces are gaining more power as the time of the tribulation approaches. The faith and prayers of My people are also growing weak in this time. Be consistent in your prayers, and do everything that you can to reach out to souls to save them from hell."*

Later, at the Eternal Father prayer group at Holy Name Adoration I could see a new bishop walking down from the altar, after being installed. Jesus said: *"My people, your present bishop will be retiring soon, and you need to keep praying for a good bishop who will allow your mission to continue. Pray that this new bishop will encourage Adoration and take a more active role in deciding who would be good candidates for the priesthood. Many good candidates have been refused, and they had to go elsewhere. Pray also for a new bishop who would be more outspoken for Right to Life causes."*

I could see some large shovels mining ore for various metal commodities. Jesus said: *"My people, the one world people and your central bankers are set on a policy to lower the value of your dollar, as they have started by buying more of your Treasury Notes. This is a false attempt to help your economy, and instead it will add to your National Debt, and result in a road to higher prices of goods with rampant inflation. The value of your commodities is not changing, but it is the value of the dollar that is decreasing relative to other currencies. This is one more step closer to your eventual bankruptcy in America."*

I could see a huge cruise ship dead in the water. Jesus said: *"My people, this latest cruise ship fire resulted in the generators burning out, which left everyone without any electricity and only emergency lighting. Stored food quickly became uneatable as the refrigeration stopped working. Air conditioning and other pumps also did not work. This having no electricity will also be a small problem at My refuges when you will have less comforts in a more rustic living. There are older means of preparing food, making soap, cleaning clothes, and providing heat in the winter. All of your raw materials will be multiplied to provide for your food, heat, and other needs. Trust in Me to protect you at My refuges from the evil ones who will be trying to kill you."*

I could hear some alarms ringing and sirens blowing to warn people of coming danger. Jesus said: *"My people, when you have tornadoes, you hear sirens warning the people to take cover. When you hear smoke alarms at night, you are warned to evacuate from a fire. Even some have carbon monoxide alarms to warn of any toxic condition. There will be another warning sign that I will wake up My faithful with at the time it is necessary to leave for My refuges. When you see a national bankruptcy, a pandemic deadly virus, mandatory chips in the body, or national martial law declared, these are the reasons for coming to My refuges. Do not hesitate to leave your homes when I warn you because your time to leave will be limited. You will not be returning to your homes, and you will be at My refuges throughout the whole tribulation. If you do not leave your homes, you will risk being captured and killed by the men in black."*

I could see farm tractors and vehicles used for planting and harvesting crops. Jesus said: *"My people, some of My refuges will be working farms that will provide fresh vegetables and various sources of meat in addition to the deer meat. Working on farms and growing feed for the animals is hard work that will require everyone's help for the refuge community to survive. You will be protected from the evil ones, and I will multiply your fuels and food that you grow. You will need fuel for your farm vehicles, for cooking, lighting, and heating. Have no fear of this time, but My faithful will be hard at work at My refuges, as well as spending more time in prayer."*

I could see life on a refuge where people had to deal with waste materials and outhouses. Jesus said: *"My people, at the refuges there will be no garbage pickups and very little running water. You will need to burn or bury your refuse, or use it for mulch. Outhouses will require maintenance as in the past with lime and landfills. This part of your life will not change, but your disposal methods will be as in older days. This lifestyle of a simpler life will bring you closer to Me, as you will have more time for prayer."*

I could see people honoring all of the military and those who died at war. Jesus said: *"My people, this feast day of St. Martin of Tours honors a saint who was first in the military before he became a cleric. This Veterans' Day also honors those in the military who have defended your freedoms in the wars with other nations. It is unfortunate that man cannot live in peace with each other. The one world people encourage wars to make their blood money on selling weapons. These evil ones will have to suffer My justice at their judgment. Continue to pray for peace and encourage peaceful solutions over war that has no winners."*

Friday, November 12, 2010:

At St. John the Evangelist after Communion I could feel a sense of ominous judgment and destruction at the return of Jesus. Jesus said: *"My people, in the next few weeks you will see the readings focused on the end days where there will be much destruction. The Gospel speaks of the people killed in the flood and those killed in the fire and brimstone of Sodom and Gomorrah. Just as My justice was brought down on the evil people of Noah's time and the evil people of Lot's time, so you will again see My justice brought down on the Antichrist and his minions. Evil under the Antichrist during the tribulation will be the worst evil that you have ever seen. Once you see the Antichrist come to power, know that My coming on the clouds to defeat him, is not far away. I will bring a fiery comet into the Atlantic Ocean that will destroy two-thirds of humanity. This will be the end of the Antichrist's power, as he and all the evil ones will be cast into hell. During the tribulation, My faithful will be protected at My refuges, and the evil ones will not be able to see them or kill them. Even when the comet comes, I will lift them up so they will not be killed. Some faithful will be martyred, but those at My refuges will be rewarded in My Era of Peace and in heaven."*

Later, at St. Theodore's tabernacle I could see an all black horse come running at me with a rider who was one of the four horsemen of the Book of Revelation. Jesus said: *"My people, I have mentioned before that you were living in the time of the red horse that had a rider with a bow meaning a time of a bloody war. Today, I am showing you a black horse which is when you are living now. This black horse has a rider who is carrying a scales, and this signifies a time of famine. I have told you before to store up one year's supply of food for the day of the world famine, and in case you do not have the chip in the body to buy your food. There are going to be an increasing number of disasters that may cause food shortages. Remember that you are now dependent on China for more than half of your food, as well as many of your other store items. With your decreasing dollar, your food will become more costly, as well as your gasoline. This world famine will be a manipulated food shortage, so it would be wise to have your own food supply in your basement. Once it is dangerous because mobs will be searching for food, it will again be another reason to leave for your refuges. It is one thing to share food with others, but when they want to kill you for it, it will be time to leave. At My refuges you will have food, water, and daily Communion provided, so do not worry that you will not have enough to eat. Trust in Me to have your guardian angels lead you to My nearest place of refuge where you will be safe from the evil ones."*

Saturday, November 13, 2010: (St. Frances Xavier Cabrini)
At the Carmelite Monastery after Communion I could see some nuns praying and the people praying at Mass. Jesus said: *"My people, today's Gospel is about the persistent widow who was begging the dishonest judge to rule in her favor. He relented in her favor for fear that she would bring physical harm to him. There was another reading about*

charity where a man was begging another at night for three loaves of bread for his guests. The one inside was reluctant at first, but later got up to give him the bread because of the visitor's persistence. So it is when you come to Me with your prayer intentions. Some are answered right away, while others may take years of persistent prayer because of the high price for that person's soul. Even at times the answer to your prayer may be a 'no', as your priest suggested. I know what is best for your soul, so I answer prayers that will best help you, or the souls that you are praying for. You are at a Carmelite monastery where the nuns are praying constantly in silence for the sinners of the world. Your world is full of so much evil that your prayers are needed every day. This decline in faith is another sign of the end times, and it is why I asked the question: 'Will I find any faith on the earth when I return?'"

Sunday, November 14, 2010:

At Holy Name after Communion I could see a long path as a person's life. Jesus said: *"My people, I want everyone to be conscious of the preparations that you need to make in case you die suddenly, or when the time of tribulation falls upon you. You do not have tomorrow until I grant it to you, so you should always have your soul in the state of grace by frequent Confession. In addition to the day of your death, people should also be ready for the time of tribulation under the Antichrist. Most people do not understand that this event could happen in their lifetime, as I have informed My son in My messages. I have talked of having one year's supply of food on hand for the coming famine, and many messages on preparing backpacks, tents, and blankets for leaving for My refuges. You will have the Warning first, a world famine, division in My Church, mandatory chips in the body, and martial law. When you see these things, call on Me and I will have your guardian angels lead you to My nearest refuge. Many priests and deacons avoid talking of the end times at this time of year, but they are doing a disservice to their people by not warning them of the coming tribulation. You need to have eyes of faith to see that you are living in the end time signs of the Bible. Those, who are left in their homes, may be captured and killed if they do not realize that they need to leave for My refuges."*

Later, at St. Theodore's tabernacle I could see a properly prepared tunnel that curved to the right. I then saw a security person and a picture of the Denver airport where more tunneling was underway. Jesus said:

"My people, the one world people are having a massive tunnel building program underway to protect themselves from something big coming up. They are also storing supplies in their VIP underground cities. This means that they are planning on some riots for a food famine, a dollar crash, or a deadly virus attack. They feel whatever they are planning, that they will be safe underground, while those, who are above ground, will be at risk for their lives. If a martial law chaos began, they would also be protected from the foreign troops who would implement any capture of citizens. By the fast tempo of this building campaign, you are being given a sign of what the one world people will be doing in their bid for taking over America. Despite all of their plans, I will warn My faithful when it is time for them to come to My refuges of protection, where the evil ones cannot harm them. Have trust in My help and protection throughout the whole time of the tribulation before I return."

Monday, November 15, 2010: (St. Albert the Great)
At St. John the Evangelist after Communion I could see Jesus calling me to write down His words to prepare the people for His coming. Jesus said: *"My people, in the*

first reading from the Book of Revelation, St. John is called to write down the words for the seven churches. He is writing in Patmos what the angel is revealing to him. In the vision My son, John, also is being called to write down My words to prepare the people for the tribulation of the Antichrist, and My coming in victory. This is a glorious time to be alive, as My son is continuing the work of his namesake in St. John. You are preparing a second DVD to alert the people when to leave for My refuges, where to go, and the many miracles of protection that I will perform in addition to multiplying food and shelters. Continue to pray your novena prayers of St. Therese so you will be protected from any attacks on your work from the evil one. This DVD will be a great help in explaining what is needed on your way to the refuges, and it is a message of hope and My mercy instead of gloom and doom. This preparation message is needed because many people do not understand that this tribulation is most likely in their lifetimes and not far off. Continue, My people, to pray and discern how to prepare for this time. By prayer and frequent Confession, you will have your soul pure and ready to meet Me at any time."

Later, at St. Theodore's tabernacle I could see a large twenty-foot bookcase of one person's records if the digital records were placed on paper. Jesus said: *"My people, most of you are unaware of the thorough records that the one world people are keeping on you. They have super computers with enough memory to store your life's history. They know all of your bank records, stocks, bonds, and real estate that you own. So they know your total worth, and they can even profile you by your credit card purchases. They have every transaction that you ever made, and they have your e-mails and phone calls recorded. Every part of your life is known to them through their unknown tapping of your communications. This is not enough control for them, but they are working on smart cards in your licenses, and you may have chips in your passports. You can protect your identity and tracking by storing any chipped documents with aluminum foil. Once the new Health Plan is implemented, these same one world people will try to demand mandatory chips in the body, so they can track you and control you with voices and mind control. Refuse to take any chips in the body, and when the evil ones try to force these on people, it will be time to go to My refuges. As you see these things coming about in front of you, you know the tribulation is very close. Fear not the evil one's plans, because you will have complete protection at My refuges where I will provide for your needs."*

Tuesday, November 16, 2010: (St. Margaret of Scotland)
At Holy Name after Communion I could see some large brown insulators at a large transformer station. Jesus said: *"My people, America's*

Achilles heel is your dependence on your electricity. Your electricity producing plants also require natural gas or coal to keep them running. These plants or any place along the transmission lines are vulnerable to accidents, bad weather, aging, and terrorism. You have seen ice storms, a car crashing into a pole, and even animals eating the line insulation where your electricity was stopped. This can also be shut down by those who control your electric grid, and by any unusual surges in the grid. You are most vulnerable in the winter, since your heaters would stop, and you would need an alternate source of heat. You also would need oil lamps for light, gas for cooking, and possibly bailing water from your sump pump. Refrigerators would not work, and you would need backup food supplies. Your gasoline pumps would also be shut down, limiting your means of travel. All of these resulting shutdowns show you the areas where you need some backups when you lose your electricity. Be prepared for this incident and possibly living without electricity at your rustic refuges. Once you come to My refuges, you will be living a much simpler life under My protection. Controlling your electricity will be one of the one world people's means of trying to force you to accept their new world order. Refuse their threats and chips in the body, and trust in My protection from the evil ones at My refuges."

Later, at St. Theodore's Adoration I could see a priest on the altar facing toward the altar and it appeared that he was offering a Latin Mass in a beautiful dalmatic attire. Jesus said: *"My people, I am showing you this vision of a Latin Mass because soon there will be a more traditional translation of the original Latin Mass. At this time it is hard for you to know what form this will take until you can view a copy. Some are saying that they do not want to change, while others want to see it before making any judgment. It is not known whether the Gospel and Epistle readings will be changed or not. You may want to do some research into finding a copy. If it is available, you can see what will be recommended at all of the churches. The last change dealt with inclusive language, so it will be a change that may take some getting used to. Pray that there will be unity over this change and not any division."*

Wednesday, November 17, 2010: (St. Elizabeth of Hungary)
At Holy Name after Communion I could see people at the judgment before God and how they were being judged. Jesus said: *"My people, in the Gospel accounts there were several versions of My parable about the*

talents or gold coins. Two of the people in the parable, who were given money, were industrious to make more money, but the third man hid the money in the ground or in a handkerchief. This is an example in life of whether you used your talents for My glory, or you wasted your talents by not using them for what they were intended. Those, who did not use their talents, may suffer longer in purgatory. The other people mentioned, who rejected the king or killed his servants, are those who committed sins, but did not repent, and they are the ones who were sent to hell because they rejected Me. You all have choices in life because I do not force you to love Me. But at the judgment you must answer and suffer the consequences of your decisions. Those, who love Me and follow My Commandments, may be purified and come to heaven. Those, who reject Me, do not keep My Commandments, and do not repent, are those who will be sent into the flames of hell. I am merciful, but I am also a just judge. I want My people to love Me and follow Me without fear. Then I will welcome you into My Wedding Banquet in heaven as your reward."

(Rosaria Proia wake) At the Bean Funeral Home in front of the casket I could see a vision of family members at Rose's bedside. Jesus said: *"My people, it is appropriate to be praying the rosary for a mother and grandmother with the name Rosaria. She has had the gift of more years than most people, but they were very productive years. When I called her home, she was ready to see Me. She will be doing a short purification in purgatory, and when her Masses are said, she will be released to be with Me in heaven. She did not leave you completely because she loves her family, and she will be praying for all of you. She will be missed at your holiday celebrations, but remember her in your prayers, especially when you give thanksgiving at your meals."* 1¥1¥1¥1¥1¥1¥1¥1¥1¥1¥1

Later, at St. Theodore's Adoration I could see myself walking in a park with the leaves on the ground, and the bright sun shining down on everything. Jesus said: *"My people, if you truly love Me, you will seek out learning everything you can about Me and My creation. When you are having a nature walk, you are joyful to be alive so you can appreciate the fall foliage, the birds, the deer, and the squirrels on your path. There is beauty in nature and in My people where you can find an extension of My love. In all of the world the souls of My people are My most prized possessions. I give you all free will so you can come to love Me by yourselves without Me forcing you. I allow the good and the bad to live their lives together, just as I spoke of the wheat and the tares growing up together. At the harvest the wheat I separated to go into My barn, while the tares were bundled together and thrown into the fire. So it is at the judgment. My faithful, who have loved Me and performed good works for others, will see their reward in heaven. The evil ones, who have killed My people and refused to repent of their sins, will be cast into the*

fires of hell. I love everyone, but those who deny life in the womb, kill older people in euthanasia, and encourage killing in wars and by viruses, are the evil ones who will face My justice. I am the giver and taker of life, and those, who deny My plans for souls by killing, are committing the worst offense against Me. Pray for these souls to change their ways before it is too late to save them from hell. I strive to have every soul come to heaven, but the evil one is battling with Me for every soul. My joy is to see My faithful evangelize and convert souls to My Gospel. If you saw how much souls suffer in the flames of hell, you would strive also to save as many souls as you could from going to hell."

Thursday, November 18, 2010:
(Dedication of Basilicas of St. Peter and St. Paul)
At Holy Name after Communion I could see a dark prison cell and a scene of when St. Paul fell off his horse at his conversion. Jesus said: *"My people, in today's feast of the Dedication of the Basilicas of St. Peter and St. Paul in Rome, you are honoring the two great pillars of My Church. St. Peter was very impulsive to act even in attempting to walk on water, but his faith was weak at times before he received the gifts of the Holy Spirit. He was the leader of My apostles, and he is represented by the many Popes in his succession. St. Paul also was a strong man in his principles, and his conversion was miraculous. I visited him personally to change him from Saul to Paul, and to change him into one of*

My greatest missionaries. Many people have visited the places where St. Paul taught in Greece and Turkey. The vision of a dungeon prison is the place where they both were imprisoned, chained, and later martyred for their faith. These two basilicas are great remembrances of

these saints where they are buried in Rome. Give praise and glory to your Lord because I have raised up My Church on the humble beginnings of these two great saints."

Later, at the Eternal Father prayer group at Holy Name Adoration I could see some large cartoon balloons that are used in parades. Jesus said: *"My people, your media has censored your news so much that they have you concentrate on issues of little importance while the important issues are overlooked or purposely avoided. Many of your freedoms are being suppressed by hate crimes and your Patriot laws. Even the latest airport security is going beyond reasonable searches. Decisions about wars and letting the Federal Reserve bankers control your finances, are never debated. Pray for your new representatives to change the socialist leanings of your current government."*

I could see people traveling in their cars without realizing how their freedom to travel will become more restricted. Jesus said: *"My people, your highways are being more controlled with easy chip passes, cameras, and North American Union special highways. Even your fuels and car regulations are becoming more expensive and controlled with chipped driver's licenses. It will come to a point where it will be difficult without chips to even travel on the main interstate highways. This is why when you go to My refuges, your angels will lead you down local roads instead of the highways."*

I could see the proceedings in Congress and those in state government. Jesus said: *"My people, your state governments have to live within balanced budgets, which means cutting employees and expenditures to match what is collected in taxes. This is contrasted with your Congress that is spending and borrowing money with no concern for balancing their budget. If they did try to achieve a balanced budget, they would have to cut outrageous salaries, too many people, and unfunded payments to Social Security, Medicare, Medicaid, Welfare, and many other payments that you cannot afford. Continued deficit spending is the one world people's means of bankrupting America. If balanced budgets are not achieved, then you could see the end of your country and your freedoms. The evil ones want to control you with microchips, so refuse them in any attempts at mandatory chips in the body."*

I could see a bridge that was carried away by an overflowing river from heavy rainfall. Jesus said: *"My people, as winter draws near, you could be seeing more natural disasters from major snow storms, ice storms, and high winds. This vision of a bridge being washed out is an example of floods from heavy rainfall. Be prepared for power outages, and food and fuel shortages by stocking up on some extra food and fuel. These items will become more expensive relative to the shrinking value of your dollar. This will become more of a hardship on people who are just getting by. You may have to help your neighbor more by supporting your local food shelves for the poor."*

I could see people sitting down for their Thanksgiving Dinner. Jesus said: *"My people, every year many families travel to their parents' home for their Thanksgiving Dinner. It is good for families to keep together in their traditions. As you are thinking of family and thanking Me for your blessings, now you are hearing statistics of how nearly half of your people are in favor of living together without marriage. Your family of husband and wife should be the model for your society, and not just relationships of convenience without responsibilities to Me and your children. The traditional family is more God centered, but your society is turning more materialistic rather than spiritual. This trend also will lead your country to ruin because of your abortions and sexual sins. Pray for your people to wake up to the immorality in your society, and change your ways to follow Me in prayer."*

I could see some people coming to Mass on the Holy Days, but they are not always present at Sunday Mass. Jesus said: *"My people, the faith of many people is growing more lukewarm as they are skipping their prayers and are not coming to Sunday Mass. You are seeing churches closing around you because many are not living their faith as they should. Yes, there are priest shortages, but it is your loss of Sunday Mass attendance that is the worst problem. My faithful need to be building up their faith on their way to perfection, instead of falling into lax spiritual habits. Your love for Me should be burning strong, but unless you pray daily, it will continue to become lukewarm. In the Bible it says how I vomit the lukewarm from My mouth. I want My faithful to be vibrant in their faith and not nearly dead spiritually."*

I could see people getting ready to put up their Christmas decorations as Advent approaches. Jesus said: *"My people, even as you are preparing for Thanksgiving, your shopkeepers are planning for Christmas selling. As you approach your coming Advent season, this is another time, as in Lent, when you plan to do a little more prayer and fasting. In days past you used to have even more Sundays of preparation for*

Advent. As you prepare again for another celebration of Christmas, think of giving Me some spiritual bouquets of prayers to help sinners and those souls in purgatory."

Friday, November 19, 2010:
At St. John the Evangelist after Communion I could see Jesus with a whip for the money changers in the Temple. Jesus said: *"My people, I love My churches because it is where I reside in My tabernacles as you come to worship Me. You should treasure your local church as well and work to keep them open by your presence, and your financial and spiritual support. My people need to be strong in their faith and do not become lukewarm. Pray to Me every day and not just one hour on Sunday. Live your faith in your works and deeds so that everyone can recognize you as a Christian. Your love for Me will be your passport when you reach the gates of heaven."*
Later, at St. Elizabeth Ann Seton's Church, Emmitsburg, Maryland after Communion I could see some of her work in teaching students and helping the sick. Jesus said: *"My people, the most important work, that you could perform, is being able to bring souls to conversion. This is why St. Elizabeth's work in teaching students their faith and other studies was so important in forming the spiritual lives of her students. You also helped teach your students how to pray the rosary in their religion class. When you bring Me closer to these students, you are a model of faith to follow. Be grateful for the opportunity to teach children their faith, and how to depend on Me for everything. Parents and teachers have a great responsibility to lead their children's souls, and point them toward heaven for their eternal destination. As you come closer to your Thanksgiving Day holiday, remember to share your wealth and your faith with the physical poor, and those who are in need of spiritual support. Also, continue to give Me thanks every day for your gift of life, and another opportunity to do more good works for Me in your neighbor's need."*

Saturday, November 20, 2010:
At Our Lady of Angels Church, Woodbridge, Virginia after Communion I could see some collapsed gold altars that signified the collapse of America. Jesus said: *"My people, in these last weeks of the Church Year, there are many readings from the Book of Revelation and other*

places that speak of the end days before My return. In order for the Antichrist to come to power, America will be taken over by the one world people. They are promoting their new world order as a world government of all the nations of the world. The vision shows the destruction of your government as you know it today, and it will be ruled by the Antichrist during the tribulation of evil. Once you see martial law and mandatory chips in the body coming, My faithful need to call on Me to have your guardian angels lead you to My refuges of protection. There My angels will shield you from the evil ones and their ruthless tyranny. Those, who refuse to leave their homes, could face martyrdom for not taking any chips in the body. The joy at the end of the tribulation is that I will come in victory with My Comet of Chastisement, and all the evil ones will be cast into hell. Then I will renew the earth and bring My faithful into My Era of Peace. My people know the end of the story and the Antichrist loses, while heaven and My angels are triumphant. This is why My message of the end days gives you hope for those who are faithful to Me."

Sunday, November 21, 2010: (Christ the King)
At the Wyndham Garden Hotel, Philadelphia, Pennsylvania after Communion I could see an overflowing number of people at Mass. Jesus said: *"My people, My love is flowing out over all of My people as My cup is overflowing with My graces and mercies for them from My Divine Mercy. I have showed you how much I love you by dying for all of you on the cross. I ask My people to love Me also by their own free will. This focus on Me should be a part of your love for Me every day in all that you do. I am your King and I should be the center of your life. Pray to Me every day and ask My help in all of your work and decisions. When you ask My help, you will see that all of your work will go well with you."*

Monday, November 22, 2010: (St. Cecilia)
At St. Margaret Mary Alacoque Church, Essington, Pennsylvania after Communion I could see a curtain of flames all around the altar during Mass. Jesus said: *"My people, this curtain of fire all around an ongoing Mass represents the coming persecution of the tribulation. Even as St. Cecilia was martyred, there will be more martyrs as the evil ones of this age will be trying to kill all of the faithful Christians*

for their new world order. In the early years of My Church there were many martyred for their faith. During the tribulation of the Antichrist this reign of terror will again be testing My people all over the earth. Those, who are martyred, will become instant saints, but the rest of My people will be protected at My refuges. Even if you are threatened by death, never give up your faith in Me. Any people who may be martyred for My sake, I will ease their pain because I never test you beyond what you could endure. Give praise and thanks to Me for all that I do for you. I will warn My people when it is time to leave for My refuges before the evil ones come to your houses. Leave by nightfall, and My angels will shield you by making you invisible. Take your backpacks, tents, and blankets as you follow your guardian angels to My nearest refuge. Honor My saints who have given their lives up for Me, rather than giving up their faith."

Later, at St. Theodore's tabernacle I could see a cemetery and there was a vase of flowers on a grave. Jesus said: *"My people, all people know that one day they will die and be placed in a grave. You have been to many funerals, so it is easy to imagine yourself in a casket at the end of your life. This may be the end of your mortal body, but it is not the end of your immortal soul. This is why it is so important to point your destination to heaven for your soul. I will do the judging, but if you follow My Commandments and repent of your sins, you are promised your reward in heaven. Work every day on minimizing your sins and maximizing your efforts to convert sinners, and do good works for your neighbor. When you have your soul constantly cleansed of your sins at monthly Confession, you will not have any fear of dying because you know your destination will be with Me in heaven."*

Tuesday, November 23, 2010: (Bl. Miguel Pro)

At St. John the Evangelist after Communion I could see the Swiss guards guarding the Vatican and the Pope. Jesus said: *"My people, as you see the Swiss guards guarding the Vatican and the Pope, so My faithful need to guard their faith and stand up for My Gospel teachings even if they are threatened with death. Never give up your faith, even as the martyrs of My Church gave up their lives instead of giving up their faith. You may not be tested with your lives, but it takes courage to fight against abortion, living together outside of marriage, and homosexual marriages. The accepted sins of your society are what will bring America to its knees from My justice. Reach out in faith to be models of good Christians both for your family and those around you. You may be persecuted for taking unpopular stands, but you are witnessing My Gospel teachings and My Ten Commandments. Use your witness to convert souls to Christianity and keep them from being lost in hell. Pray for all of your family members so they can be saved. By guarding your faith for yourself and others in your evangelization efforts, you will have your reward in heaven."*

Later, at St. Theodore's Adoration I could see a king and queen dressed in all of their finery. Jesus said: *"My people, there are some kings and queens in the world, but they are usually just titles without much authority. You just celebrated My Kingship which is more inclusive than any*

human king. I am your Master and Creator to whom you should give honor and thanks for creating you. Kings and queens have subjects that are bound to obey them. I am a King, but I do not force My love on people. I give all of you free will so you can come to love Me of your own free choice. Once you choose to love Me, I should be your Master and the center focus of your life. I give you everything to survive, and I died for your sins so you could be saved to come to heaven. As you celebrate Thanksgiving Day, remember to thank Me for all that you have been given, especially the gifts of life in your family. You remembered those who have died this year, but you also should remember how fortunate you are to have a loving family to comfort you in this hard life on earth. I love all of you so much, and I guide you on your path to heaven."

Wednesday, November 24, 2010: (Vietnamese martyrs)
At Holy Name after Communion I could see several large Vs representing the victory of Jesus over the Antichrist and Satan. Jesus said: *"My people, in these end time readings there is much talk of persecution and killing of martyrs, but this evil is balanced by the promise of My victory in the end. I am much more powerful than anything that the evil ones could do on earth. There will be a time of tribulation as described in the Book of Revelation, but this time will be less than 3 ½ years for the sake of My elect. There is always a battle between good and evil, but at the end, the evil ones are cast into hell, while My faithful are brought into My Era of Peace. I will protect My faithful at My refuges, but some will be martyred for their faith. The descriptions of heaven are glorious in these readings, so have no fear and have peace in your soul as My faithful await their entry into heaven. Your time in My Era of Peace and then in heaven will be your reward for being faithful to loving Me and following My Commandments."*

Later, at St. Theodore's Adoration I could see someone shopping at a mall for some snow boots. Jesus said: *"My people, as seen in the vision, many shoppers are ready to start their Christmas shopping at their local mall stores. Your shopkeepers are hoping to see more profits this year than the last few years of recession. There are still many people who are unemployed, and their unemployment checks are running out. People are preparing for another winter season by buying snow boots, hats, gloves, and scrappers for their cars. Heavier coats are also needed as snow storms are causing blizzards in the Middle Northern states. Some people even migrate to warmer states for the winter. Longer nights and getting close to the winter solstice are other signs of winter's arrival. Pray for good weather for your families that are traveling for their Thanksgiving meetings. Your Mid-Atlantic states had some heavy snow storms last year, and you may see more of the same this year. Be prepared for any power outages with extra fuel sources as wood and kerosene for burners in addition to your natural gas burners. Having some extra food and oil for your lamps will also keep you eating with sufficient light. Give thanks to Me in your prayers before your dinner, and enjoy exchanging conversations with your relatives who you do not see very often."*

Thursday, November 25, 2010: (Thanksgiving Day)
At Holy Name after Communion I could see people walking among some tall trees in a forest. Jesus said: *"My people, today is the day for a special thank you to Me for all that I have given you. You were fortunate to be born in America where you still have more freedoms than some countries. This vision of My creation in the forests is how you can thank Me for all the beautiful nature scenes around you. You have your life, your faith, and your beautiful family, if you are married with children. Your society is slowly drifting into a pagan style of living when people look down on marriage as unnecessary. I know many women can be independent financially with their own jobs, but living in marriage is also following My Commandments, compared to living together in a sinful environment. This is not just a casual opinion, but a moral lifestyle is much more expected of My faithful than living in fornication or in homosexual relationships. You should also be thankful for your job, if you have one, and all of your possessions. The best way that you could thank Me for My gifts is when you share your wealth with those who are poor, and to even share your faith in bringing souls to conversion. Your Thanksgiving Dinner is a pleasure for eating, but also it is a time to share your conversation with relatives and friends. You can also reach out to people by praying for their health and their needs. Thank you also for those who came to Mass to give Me thanks. I encourage all of you to share your love with Me and your neighbors."*

Friday, November 26, 2010:
At St. John the Evangelist after Communion I could see a small hole dug in the ground for a mechanical water pump at a well of spring water. Jesus said: *"My people, an independent water source will be needed at every refuge for water to drink, for cooking, and for bathing. As in the vision, a mechanical pump would be desired because most refuges will not have any electricity. At times it may be difficult to have such a well because of your zoning regulations for pure water. When water*

is needed, I will see to it that your wells will not run dry. *For those refuges that have not secured such a water source, I will allow a spring to develop to supply My people with the water they need. Such spring water will also have miraculous healing properties for all of your sicknesses. Trust in Me that I will protect My faithful at My refuges, and I will provide you with all that you need both physically and spiritually. Be ready when I will warn you that it is time to leave for My refuges."*

Later, at St. Theodore's tabernacle I could see a large water fountain with a spray going almost to the roof inside a church. Jesus said: *"My people, this fountain of water is a sign that My faithful need constant cleansing of their sins in frequent Confession. I have told you before that most of the sexual sins are usually mortal sins. Fornication, adultery, and birth control are in this realm of mortal sins. My Church has taught for years that every marital act needs to be open to the possibility of new life without being obstructed. This is why vasectomies, tubal ligations, artificial insemination, and condoms all have as their intent the manipulation of life for convenience. All forms of birth control are therefore serious sins, no matter what particular condition could be posed. Once you start making exceptions to these laws of the Sixth Commandment, then you are treading on dangerous territory."*

Saturday, November 27, 2010:

At St. John the Evangelist after Communion I could see a road with candles on both sides that signified a waiting for Jesus' return. Jesus said: *"My people, this is the last day of the Church Year, and you are seeing more references to the end times of My return in the readings. In the vision you are seeing a vigil with candles on a road, as you await My return. You are to continue on with your life's work every day, but you can still have a pure soul that is ready to meet Me when I return. It is better to be prepared for the end times as the five wise virgins who had their oil and lamps ready, than the five foolish virgins who did not. My faithful also need to be ready to leave your homes for My refuges with your backpacks ready, and all of your preparations for the tribulation. As you keep a light or candle lit at your home altar, let this be your vigil candle that awaits My return."*

Later, at St. Theodore's tabernacle I could see different teams playing various sports. Jesus said: *"My people, the one common thread through most of your sports games is that you always have two opposing sides.*

j. TERELYA

You also have different numbers of players in different sports. The battle between good and evil also has two sides, but any number of players. On the good team you have the Three Persons of the Blessed Trinity with more power than the evil side of Satan, the demons, and the Antichrist. Also, on the good side you have the angels and saints, especially your own guardian angel. In the background you also have your fellow faithful, and the souls in purgatory to help in the battle against evil. You have three basic armies for good: the saints of the Church Triumphant in heaven, the souls in purgatory of the Church Suffering, and the faithful souls on earth of the Church Militant. In order to fight the good fight, you need to defend yourself with the grace of My sacraments, the breastplate of righteousness and the helmet of salvation. Be able to stand up and resist the evil one's temptations, and stand fast to your beliefs in Me no matter what you must suffer."

Sunday, November 28, 2010: (First Sunday of Advent)
At Holy Name after Communion I could see decorations for a feast day in the Holy Lands. Jesus said: *"My people, this First Sunday of Advent is similar to the Christ the King Sunday in that it calls you to 'Stay awake' and be vigilant because I could return on a day that you are not suspecting. In the Gospel it tells you that the Son of Man will return when there is evil on the earth as in the days of Noah before the flood. You are seeing more evil on the earth now, and it will even get worse during the tribulation. Know when you see the Antichrist rise to power, it will not be long before I will return in victory over him. His reign will be short for less than 3 ½ years. I want you to go about your daily tasks, but have your soul pure for the day of My return which is in your lifetime."*

Later, at St. Theodore's tabernacle I could see a priest giving his homily at Mass. Jesus said: *"My people, I have mentioned to you before how My priest sons could do more to help the people by teaching them sermons on the faith. I want to give you such a sermon on a typical day of how to show your love for Me. Not everyone can make this time for Me, but you are in control of your own time and how you plan it. In the morning when you wake up, you could spend a few moments to pray your morning offering and your guardian angel prayer. Next, you could ask Me to discern your list of activities for the day to fulfill your responsibilities to your job, your family's needs, and any tasks that require your work. As you start each project, ask for My help to do the best job possible. Show your love for Me in your actions. You usually start your day with morning Mass and Communion. Sometime later in the day you make time for Me in your three or four rosaries, and your Divine Mercy Chaplet at the 3:00 p.m. hour. You finish up your day with an Hour of Adoration in front of My Blessed Sacrament. It is at night that you can reflect on your actions of the day, and see how you could learn from your mistakes so you do not repeat them. Right before going to sleep you could recite your Act of Contrition in case you should die overnight. By paying attention to having Me be a part of all that you do, you are offering up all of your actions for My greater glory. Working on your daily love relationship with Me will keep you close to Me, and always ready to meet Me at your judgment."*

Monday, November 29, 2010:

At Holy Name after Communion I could see the roofs of some beautiful buildings from inside. Jesus said: *"My people, today's Gospel shows how much I was impressed by even a Roman centurion's faith in Me. He recognized that I had the power to heal his sick servant, but even from a distance without coming into his home. He knew that it would defile a Jew to come into his home, so he gave the famous quote that you say before Communion: 'Lord, I am not worthy that Thou should enter under my roof, but only say the word and I shall be healed.' This was an act of faith for the centurion, but when you repeat this saying, you are making your own act of faith in the healing power of My Eucharist. The consecrated Host is My Real Presence. So literally you are taking Me into the roof of your mouth. Because you are receiving Me in faith, it would be reverent to bow or genuflect to receive Me on your tongue. Faith in Me is a gift, and few believe in My Real Presence because they are not taught, or they have a difficulty in believing that I could truly be present in the Host. This requires faith to believe in the Transubstantiation of the bread and wine that are transformed into My own Body and Blood at the Consecration. The centurion believed in My miracles of healing, but My faithful are asked to believe in My miracle of being fully present in the consecrated Bread in all the tabernacles of the world."*

Later, at St. Theodore's tabernacle I could see a parked school bus at night and someone threw a stone through the back window. Jesus said: *"My people, it is bad enough to see terrorist acts on adults, but it is even worse to see attacks on young children. You have seen sexual predators prey on teenagers both at night and even through the internet. Terrorists do not care who they kill, whether people are young children, teenagers, or adults. You are seeing some terrorists recruiting teenagers and women for their cause because people would be less suspicious of them to make terrorist attacks. If you see some suspicious activity, you need to be watchful because terrorism could come from anyone at any age, or from any gender. Much of this activity is directed by Muslim extremists which is why they seek out others to do their acts of terrorism. It is hard to understand why they want to persecute Christians, but for some of them it is a part of their Islamic beliefs that drive them to kill the infidels, or those outside of their faith. There are not many serious incidents in America, but terrorist activity is spread throughout the world. Pray that your security could stop these plans before they start. Over time this persecution will worsen, so be prepared to go to My refuges when I warn you that it is time."*

Tuesday, November 30, 2010: (St. Andrew)
At Holy Name after Communion I could see an old log cabin without any electricity. Jesus said: *"My people, all of My apostles, except St. John, suffered martyrdom for their faith. St. Andrew introduced several apostles to Me as he became a fisher of men for teaching My Gospel.*

Just as My apostles and many of My early followers were persecuted by the Romans, so My faithful of today will also be facing persecution from the one world people. When you call on Me, I will have your guardian angel lead you to the nearest refuge where you will be protected by an angel that you will see. The angel will make you invisible to your enemies, and you may be staying at a log cabin as in the vision. You will need to do some hard manual labor to survive, but My refuges will protect you from the evil ones who are trying to kill you. Some will be martyred, but the rest will be saved. Many of your comforts will be taken away, but you will have more time for prayer and adoring Me in My tabernacles."

Later, at St. Theodore's Adoration I could see some kings wearing their crowns, and during the Roman occupation, I could see where the Christians hid underground in the catacombs. Jesus said: *"My people, during the first three hundred years after My death, the Romans persecuted My faithful so that many were martyred for their faith. The Romans even made sport of these killings with lions and gladiators. There is a parallel persecution of Christians going on even today. In communist countries and Muslim countries there are people killing Christians. The coming Antichrist is a Muslim leader, and he will continue this persecution of Christians. The plan of the one world people is to declare martial law and kill as many Christians and patriots as they can in their detention death camps. I will warn My people when it is time to leave for My refuges so they can avoid being killed by these evil ones. At My refuges My angels will shield you and provide for your physical and spiritual needs. Trust in Me to protect My faithful, and reward you in My Era of Peace."*

Wednesday, December 1, 2010:

At Holy Name after Communion I could see Jesus multiplying the seven loaves of bread and the fish for all the crowd to have some. Jesus said: *"My people, this sharing of bread and fish was My compassion on the crowd in their need for food. Man in his human condition requires food and water to survive. This multiplication of bread is also a parallel to Communion that I shared with My disciples at the first Mass at the Last Supper. Multiplying food is how I will feed My people during the tribulation when you are at My refuges. My angels will multiply the daily Communion that you will receive, just as the manna was provided in the Old Exodus. Any other food from farm crops or meat from animals will also be multiplied. You will even see multiplication of your dwellings so everyone will have a place to stay. You know that I can multiply things as in this Gospel, so trust in Me to multiply things that you need at My refuges. Water also will be plentiful for drinking, cooking, and bathing."*

Later, at St. Theodore's Adoration I could see a crucifix on the ground at a cemetery. Jesus said: *"My people, as you go about your daily activities, only a few people consider the possibility that they could die any day. Accidents, or a sudden heart attack could take you at any time. Just because you are healthy, it does not guarantee that you will be alive tomorrow. It is best to keep a pure soul by at least monthly Confession. When a person dies, it does not guarantee that he or she will go to heaven immediately. Of the souls that do not go to hell, most of them will require some time in purgatory. It would be good to direct someone to have Masses said for your soul in your will. Masses can release souls from purgatory more than just prayers alone. You all must die one day, so it is best to be prepared at any time. Some patients with cancer can be better prepared because they know that their time is limited. You are all terminal, but it is just a matter of when you will die. This is why it is important to try to evangelize souls before they leave this earth because you do not want anyone to be lost in hell. Reach out to save as many souls as you can while you still have time."*

Thursday, December 2, 2010:

At Holy Name after Communion I could see a large roll of twine being spooled at a factory. Jesus said: *"My people, your life is like this spool of twine being wound day after day. This also represents how vulnerable you are to death if this twine has a break. The Gospel has a very deep understanding as well, when I compared the faith of two people where one built it on rock and the other on sand. If you build your house of faith on the rock of St. Peter, then you will be able to withstand the buffets of the devil's temptations. But if you build your house of faith on sand, as only yourself, then you will be vulnerable to collapse when tempted by the devil. You need to do more than just call My Name, Lord, Lord. In order to be saved in heaven you need to follow the Will of My Father in heaven, and direct your actions to fulfill His Will. By following the Commandments of love and doing good works for your neighbor, your reward in heaven will be great."*

Later, at the Eternal Father prayer group at Holy Name Adoration I could see a child in the store picking out his Christmas gift. Jesus said: *"My people, when you have children, I know how you want to buy Christmas gifts for them. Giving gifts to your children comes from your heart because you want to make them happy. It is better to buy fewer, less expensive gifts than to spoil them by buying all that they want. Gifts to family and friends are one part of sharing, but you also need to share My coming at My birth on earth with everyone. I came to you on earth so I could die for your sins, but I also taught you the faith in My words that you read in the Bible. Give praise and glory to Me as you prepare to celebrate My birthday on Christmas."*

I could see a light on many rings of bark on a tree. Jesus said: *"My people, for many years your legislators have deceived your people by using giveaways and enhanced entitlements to win votes for election. By offering Social Security, Welfare, Medicare, and the like, the intent was to help the poor. Unfortunately, these plans, as your new Health Law, were not fully funded for what would come in the future. As a result, people have come to rely on this free money without seeing that these things are unaffordable through taxes, and they will bankrupt America without some cutbacks. Only recently are you understanding how your debts and deficits are out of control. The one world people will use your debts to bring down your country. Then your hope will only be in going to My refuges of protection."*

I could see riots in Greece and France over harsh cutbacks. Jesus said: *"My people, in Greece many rioted when they had to make serious cutbacks to get loans at good interest rates. Similar uproars have been seen in France over raising the retirement age. Also in California the students have protested higher tuition payments. Your country has been drowning in deficits so long that it will take strong medicine to reverse deficits to balanced budgets. Once these decisions are forced on you, you will see many upset people as well. If this deficit trend is allowed to continue, your years as a nation will be numbered. The plan of the evil ones is being carried out, and it will start with the crash of the dollar. Prepare for your refuges when martial law will be declared."*

I could see a politician censured in the House of Representatives. Jesus said: *"My people, it is bad enough that your politicians have nearly bankrupted your country with bailouts and entitlements. Now, you are seeing the corruption of this censured politician who used means to evade taxes and help his election funding. This is a hard example for people to trust politicians when they are even censured by their own peers. Pray to elect moral lawmakers who will support the needs of the people, and not just interest groups."*

I could see a row of at least ten steering wheels that control the rudder of a ship. Jesus said: *"My people, your country has too many leaders that are trying to take your country in many directions. Each group wants its own way to satisfy its own political base. It is almost impossible to get clear agreement on issues important to America because each group is seeking its own power base. Unless each side is truly willing to have compromises to run your government, then gridlock could paralyze any needed action on debts and deficits. By the time it is understood that compromise is necessary, it could be too late to save your country from the central bankers and the one world people. Pray to keep your freedoms while you still have time to change."*

I could see a large fan spinning around that showed the years of a soul's life being reviewed in the Warning. Jesus said: *"My people, there is coming a general Warning that will be a supernatural intervention of My Divine Mercy to try and save many souls. This Warning experience will be like a near death experience for everyone at the same time. I have told you that this life review will come before the Antichrist takes power, and it will prepare souls to come to My refuges. The more you see events getting close to mandated chips in the body, martial law, and more virulent viruses, this means that the Warning is close. In your Warning experience you will be warned not to take chips in the body, not to worship the Antichrist, and to prepare to go to My refuges. After the Warning you are to remove your TVs, computers, and radios from your homes so you are not controlled by the Antichrist's eyes. These events are closer than you think and not tens of years away."*

I could see someone receiving Communion and the wine that had been changed into the Blood of Jesus. Jesus said: *"My people, you are to trust in Me at all times, even if you face persecution and possible martyrdom. When you eat My Body and drink My Blood at Communion, you are promised eternal life. My faithful will find protection at My refuges no matter what the evil ones will plan against you. At My refuges you will be free of disease and have all of your needs provided for. Your body will pass away, but your soul lives on forever. Protect your soul with frequent Confession and prayer, and you will be prepared for whatever you will face in life."*

Friday, December 3, 2010: (St. Francis Xavier)
At St. John the Evangelist after Communion I could see a beautiful bright spirit of a guardian angel looking face to face with the soul whom the angel loved dearly in a spiritual way. Jesus said: *"My people, I am sharing this beautiful image of a guardian angel with the soul that the angel is protecting. The bright white spiritual color is the radiance of My grace and power in this being. The angel is face-to-face with its protected soul because there is a deep spiritual love of the angel for that soul. You know how much I love My souls because I died to redeem all of you. All spiritual beings, as saints and good angels, love you as well, even as you love them. The evil angels, or demons, are filled with hate for you, which is why they try to draw you to evil actions. Your guardian angels also have a great love for you, and they try to direct you to do good things at all times. My people should also love their guardian angels, and recite your prayer to your guardian angel every day. They are with you at all times, so acknowledge your thanks to them in helping you to save your soul. You also call on your guardian angel for favors in helping you or others. You can thank them for that help also. I know this is their job to help you, but showing them your love would be a way to thank them for loving you."*
Later, at Holy Name Divine Mercy Holy Hour I could see a beautiful gold cup with the Most Precious Blood in it, and a consecrated Host in a monstrance located on a soft violet velvet material. Jesus said: *"My people, all of My faithful adorers are blessed to have My Real Presence in My Blessed Sacrament to adore and worship. The power given to My priests to consecrate bread and wine into My Body and Blood is beyond human comprehension. This is why it is so important to guard your priests in prayer from the evil ones and to support them in their work in the parish. Do not take daily Mass for granted, because soon you will be seeing more churches closed. It eventually will come to the point where it is only safe to have secret Masses in the homes. Enjoy your Masses in your churches now because this will change dramatically when the religious persecution starts. Do whatever you can to protect My Hosts from being stolen or desecrated. Give praise and thanks to Me for giving you My Real Presence in My Eucharist."*

Saturday,
December 4, 2010

At St. John the Evangelist after Communion I could see people storing their coats at a funeral home, and then I saw the collages of pictures and awards of the deceased's life. Jesus said: *"My people, it is one thing to picture yourself in the casket of a funeral as you should be prepared to meet Me at your judgment every day. As you look at the collages of the deceased's life, you see through all the years how they fit into the family's activities. Picture your own life's collage through the years in all the good and bad experiences of your life. I am trying to get you to review your life because you are going to face your unforgiven sins in the Warning experience that is coming soon. You will be so moved by your contrition for your sins that you will truly understand how much your sins offend Me. People, who have had a near-death experience, seek Confession as quickly as possible. The Warning experience will enable you to remember every unconfessed sin in your life. You can prepare for your Warning by making a good Confession with a good review of your life beforehand. You should always be conscious of struggling to improve your perfection every year. At some point during the year, as at the end, it would be good to compare where you are now spiritually to how you were at the beginning of the year. With a good recollection of your thoughts, you could make some resolutions how to improve your life for the coming year. By working on changing your habitual sins, you could come closer to Me in your perfection. See that you improve each year instead of falling back into your old sins."*

Later, at St. Cecilia's Church tabernacle I could see arches in a round church become like flashing scenes of life in a kaleidoscope representing a life review of the Warning. Jesus said: *"My people, you recognize immediately the meaning of this spinning kaleidoscope as a part of the life review that everyone will see in their Warning experience. You also are astute to know that this is the third Warning message in the last few days which is another indication that the Warning day is getting close.* (12-4, 12-2) *I am trying to have My people prepared in their souls for what you will face in your Warning experience. By going to frequent Confession, you can minimize any unforgiven sins that will be emphasized to you in your Warning. Pray for many souls to be converted and forgiven in this Warning. My grace of forgiveness will be offered to every sinner, but I do not force My love on anyone. I will show you your sins and how much they offend Me. It is up to your free will to have a change of heart and seek My love and forgiveness. Coming in front of Me in My Light to review your life, may be a traumatic experience, but one that is necessary to wake up people out of their sinful behavior. Once you return to your bodies, you will have a strong desire for My forgiveness and a desire to make Me the Master of your life. Catholics will desire Confession to a priest, while others will seek My forgiveness in their own way. Be thankful that you are being alerted to save your soul and follow Me, instead of following the Antichrist. Do not take any chips in your body, and do not worship the Antichrist, nor look at his eyes."*

Sunday, December 5, 2010: (Second Sunday of Advent)
At Holy Name after Communion I could see St. John the Baptist crying in the desert, and at one point I could see a spray of water coming towards me. Jesus said: *"My people, this cry in the desert by St. John the Baptist was his exclamation, 'Repent', which he repeated often. He was asking those who came to repent of their sins and ask God's forgiveness. He even asked them to be baptized by immersion in the Jordan River. He ate locusts and wild honey, and wore simple clothing in the desert. His mission was to prepare the people for My coming, but not just at My birth. He was preparing the people to hear My Good News that is read now in My Gospels. He was preparing the people for the coming of the Kingdom. Many beautiful images are given in Isaiah which even describes My Era of Peace on My return. The early readings of Advent are talking of My beginning ministry when St. John is*

mentioned. In the later weeks of Advent you will be reading of My birth at Bethlehem. Many of your shoppers need to keep focused on Me in wishing each other a 'Merry Christmas' because My coming on earth is the reason for your celebration. This is not just Season's Greetings, but it is My greeting to all of you that I love you enough to become a man on earth, and die for the sins of everyone, no matter what your faith is. So repent and rejoice as you share the season of My birth at Christmas."

Later, at St. Joseph's place during the rosary I could look out from a Nativity scene at all the family members praying their rosary in the living room. Jesus said: *"My people, as you prepare your Christmas decorations, be sure to have at least one presentation of a Nativity Scene so people remember the most important part of Christmas. This vision is beautiful because you are seeing a family praying the rosary together in front of a Nativity Scene. Some of you have been fortunate to visit Bethlehem in Israel and have brought home some keepsakes of My Nativity. In this Christmas Season many people are focused on shopping for gifts, but the best gift that you could give Me is yourselves in prayer. When you are gathered around your tree and decorations, you could try to get you family to pray at least one decade of the rosary before you hand out your gifts. If your family is stronger in faith, maybe even a whole rosary could be said with the intentions for the souls of your family. By putting prayer more in focus around your gift giving, you can keep love of Me more in focus on My feast day."*

Monday, December 6, 2010: (St. Nicholas)

At St. John the Evangelist I could see a church that had been set on fire. Jesus said: *"My people, the evil ones will be getting worse in the authorities, and the religious persecution will spread to public closing of churches, or they may be destroyed by fire. This is another reason for Masses in the homes until it is time to go to My refuges. Your prayer groups would be good places to meet, but you may have to be secret about where and when to meet. This is why it would be the right time to start going to a prayer group, or forming your own prayer group. You can see how Christians are being persecuted already in the media, and this will only get worse, just as Hitler persecuted the Jews. It will be harder for Christians to hold jobs, buy food, homes, or anything else. When the authorities mandate chips in the body, or start killing Christians, then it will be time to call on Me to have your guardian angels lead you to My nearest refuge."*

Later, at St. Theodore's tabernacle I could see some men dressed in dark clothes at night, and they had a large box that they were opening which had bombs and guns. Jesus said: *"My people, many of your terrorist attacks have occurred around Christian holy days. This vision of a terrorist group is how they are plotting to blow up some crucial power stations that could cripple your electric grid in the middle of winter. Power outages are difficult to recover from, but people are more vulnerable for heating their homes, and finding food during the winter. Important grid locations should have cameras and alert security so you can prevent situations that would cause long power outages. Storms and heavy snow cause enough outages, but sabotage should be a little easier to prevent. This is another reason to have some extra food on hand with another source of heating your house as well. Being prepared for times when you are most vulnerable is the best insurance when bad things happen. Preparing your soul with frequent Confession is another insurance when I will call you home."*

Tuesday, December 7, 2010: (St. Ambrose)

At St. John the Evangelist after Communion I could see people who had cleared the high snow off of their roofs. Jesus said: *"My people, already in some places in your Northern states you are seeing two feet of snow on everything. This has caused some highway blockages and a few short power outages. Enough snow on the roof can melt and form icicles which can cause water leaks or damage to the roof with enough weight of the snow. This is why after heavy snows, some people shovel the snow off the roof as a precaution. Keeping a clean driveway or a clear roof can have an analogy in the spiritual world to keeping a clean soul by Confession. In your secular world you like to be able to drive out of your driveway, especially for emergencies. In your spiritual world it is even more important to keep your soul pure in case I call you home in death. Your soul is even more important than your body which will pass away, but your soul lives on forever. During Advent as you prepare for Christmas, you need to focus more on your prayers and frequent Confession so you can present your spiritual gifts to Me at My crib."*

Later, at St. Theodore's Adoration I could see a large expanse of ocean water off the shore. Jesus said: *"My people, I have given you many messages on the need for fresh water because it is so necessary for survival, but only three percent of the earth's water does not contain salts. I have mentioned the need for fresh water sources at all of My refuges. I will see to it that all refuges have sufficient fresh water for survival and the wells will not run dry. Water will be multiplied where needed. You have seen problems with pollution and people stealing water for bottling purposes. One of the solutions for increasing fresh water supplies is the use of membrane technology where there is access to ocean water next to deserts. In the West where there are fresh water shortages, membranes could be used on ocean water off California to make more fresh water. This would come at a price people would be willing to pay for. Pray that sufficient amounts of fresh water can be provided for all peoples all over the world."*

Wednesday, December 8, 2010: (Immaculate Conception)
    At Holy Name after Communion I could see the Blessed Virgin Mary crushing the head of the serpent. Jesus said: *"My people, you know how I had prepared My Blessed Mother for her role in bringing a Redeemer for My people into this world. From her very conception she was blessed to have no original sin on her soul. She was to continue throughout her*

whole life to be sinless so she would be a perfect Ark of the Covenant to carry Me for nine months until My birth. Her Immaculate Heart has always been joined with My Sacred Heart. My Blessed Mother is also a gift to all humanity as your spiritual mother. She encourages all of her children to pray her rosary which contains quotations from Scripture in the prayers. This feast is also a National feast because she is patroness of America under her title of the 'Immaculate Conception'. The basilica in her honor in Washington, D.C. is testimony to her place as your Holy Mother. Give thanks to My Blessed Mother for placing her mantle of protection over all of her children."

Later, at St. Theodore's Adoration I could see a modern new LCD TV and part of it was pulled away to show a netting behind the screen. Jesus said: *"My people, your televisions have mesmerized your people into believing what is said over and over until you are brainwashed to believe the one world people's line. The netting behind the screen shows the TV is dragging people into wasting a lot of their time. There are a few good religious programs, but there are more violent, and promiscuous movies and programs which are sending the wrong message to your young people. You should limit your TV watching to no more than one hour a day, or your children will become dependent on it as a babysitter. Use of the internet on your computers is another source of violence and pornography. Some sites can even cause marriage breakups. This also should be limited in the time you are on it. You can see why it will be necessary to remove these image sources once the Antichrist controls the channels. Especially after the Warning, remove your TVs and computers from your homes so you do not look at the Antichrist's eyes or listen to his voice where he could control your mind. Be aware of possible addictions with TV watching and use of the internet. Pray for My help so you are focused more on spiritual things than worldly things."*

Thursday, December 9, 2010: (St. Juan Diego)

At Holy Name after Communion I could see the 'Holy Grail' relic that had the Body and Blood of Jesus in it at the Last Supper. Jesus said: *"My people, you are aware of many relics of My time during My mission on earth. Some have small pieces of My cross, the spear of Longinus, the crown of thorns, and the veil of Veronica. One of the more treasured relics was one they called the 'Holy Grail' which I used at the Last Supper for the bread and wine that I consecrated into My Body and Blood. This suffering and death on the cross was My ransom for the sins of all mankind, and it was the reason that I came as a man on the earth. This Advent Season is the beginning of My life story all over again as you will be celebrating My birth on Christmas. There are many peoples that honor My infancy with their novenas and traditions. Give praise and thanks to your Lord who loves you so much that I was willing to die for your salvation."*

Later, at the Eternal Father prayer group at the Holy Name Adoration I could see a lot of metallic debris falling to earth from a broken up satellite. Jesus said: *"My people, large satellites after time have their orbits drawn closer to earth until they breakup. Large pieces that survive burning up usually land in the ocean, but on occasion people mistake them for meteors. These falling satellites are watched by your military, but you are only warned if there is a risk of radiation being spread. With enough care for orbits, such vehicles could be directed to places away from inhabited areas."*

I could see a long tunnel hollowed out of a mountain for a road, but it also contained protection for military equipment. Jesus said: *"My people, you have seen many tunnels through rocky mountains to run roads and railroads. Such hardened protection could also house military equipment that could withstand even nuclear attacks. There are many such hiding places that are housing food and protection for your important authorities. Some are underground cities, but others are hidden in rocky mountains. I will protect My faithful at My refuges that also will be shielded from bombs by My angels. The one world people know they are going to meet resistance, so they are preparing these bomb shelters for their own protection."*

I could see a crucifix inside a refuge building where the faithful will come to pray and have Mass when priests are available. Jesus said: *"My people, as the persecution of the tribulation is about to start, it will become necessary to hold Masses in the homes, and prayer groups will need to meet in secret. My faithful have tabernacles, Mass kits, bread, wine, and candles ready for home Masses. Priests and My faithful will be targets for the one world people to kill, so when I give the warning to leave, then bring your priests to My refuges. When you call on Me, your guardian angels will lead you to My nearest refuge. The angels will shield you with invisibility so the evil ones cannot find you."*

I could see an image of Our Lady of Guadalupe being carried around the Americas as a sign of faith in Our Lady's miracle. Jesus said: *"My people, you are celebrating the feast of Juan Diego who presented his tilma full of flowers in front of the bishop during the winter. His tilma had a miraculous image of My Blessed Mother on it, and this was a sign that verified Juan's visions of Our Lady as real. This tilma has been a sign of My Blessed Mother's protection of all the Americas under the title of 'Our Lady of Guadeloupe'. Ask for My Blessed Mother's help in prayer, and honor her in any processions using this image."*

I could see Mary and Joseph on their way to Bethlehem. Jesus said: *"My people, it was part of My plan to use the Roman census that would draw all the Jews to their place of ancestry. This was to fulfill the passage from Micah that foretold My*

birth in the city of David at Bethlehem. (Micah 5:1) *'But you Bethlehem-Ephratha too small to be among the clans of Juda, from you shall come forth for Me one who is to be ruler in Israel..' Some called Me the Son of David because this truly is the lineage of both of My parents. See how all that was foretold about Me in the Scriptures had to be fulfilled."*

I could see rioting students in England who were protesting the tripling of their tuition expenses. Jesus said: *"My people, the riots in England were part of some austerity measures to try and help balance their budgets and cut their debts. Take a good look at this protest be-*

cause you could see such riots in America when your own Federal and State governments start cutting your overspending with entitlements in order to balance your budgets. Some are crying over no Social Security raises and no government employee raises. What will happen when pensions and other entitlements cannot be paid because there is not enough money to pay the people. Truly you could have riots which is why the one world people are ready with their underground cities that would protect the elite from harm. Trust in Me to feed you and shelter you at My refuges."

I could see some people preparing their Santo Nino statues for doing their novenas before Christmas. Jesus said: *"My people, many Spanish*

speaking countries honor Me with a novena of prayers before Christmas. Some of you have Santo Nino statues of My infancy at your home altars. By praying this novena, you could have the souls of your family as your intention to pray for. You could also do this novena as there are several on the internet to follow."

Friday, December 10, 2010:

At St. John the Evangelist after Communion I could see a trough around a mountain and there was a white gleaming substance that came down the trough that represented the graces and mercy of God. Jesus said: *"My people, in several situations with Moses at Mt. Sinai, God the Father shared graces with the people of the world in giving them the Ten Commandments. Now in the last century or so there have also been apparitions received on the mountains by young children through My Blessed Mother. The mountains have a holy aura for graces and the mercy of God that has been shared with all of mankind. Some people do not want to follow My Commandments because it makes demands of love on their lifestyles to be without sinful earthly pleasures. Those, who want to gain heaven, need to pray and follow My laws which are really guidelines of how to lead a holy life. Even the messages to the children also are a help to guide your lives to heaven. Be grateful that heaven has revealed to you the gifts of My Commandments of love and the messages of comfort from My Blessed Mother."*

Later, at St. Theodore's tabernacle I could see instigated riots resulting in a martial law, and the real targets were shipped out in box cars to be killed. Jesus said: *"My people, you have seen throughout history how those in power have created false flag* events to trigger a desired war. Part of America's problems is that Congress is no longer claiming their power to declare war. Instead the President and those desiring war are making that decision. Now in some countries as England, France, and Greece, you are seeing riots among the people over austerity changes to correct overspending. Even your talk shows are concerned that austerity changes in America could precipitate riots among interest groups. What is more concerning is if some elements of your society do not get their way with the new Congress. You could see some false flag* riots in order to declare martial law. Once martial law is invoked, the one world people will have their opportunity to force a new world order over you in forming the North American Union. If you see wholesale riots all over America, then be ready to leave for My refuges. Martial law will be a license for the one world people to kill the religious and patriots who are their real targets. Then you will see the men in black take prisoners to boxcars for extermination at their death camps. By leaving early for My refuges, you can avoid being captured by the evil authorities. Pray for My word when it is the right time to leave your homes."*

*(Note: False flag operations are covert operations designed to deceive the public in such a way that the operations appear as though they are being carried out by other entities when in fact they are the plan of the one world people.)

Saturday, December 11, 2010:
At St. John the Evangelist after Communion I could see people being tortured and killed in other countries. Jesus said: *"My people, many of My prophets were killed because they carried My message, but the worldly people did not want to hear them because the prophets criticized the evil ones' lifestyles. Even St. John the Baptist criticized Herod for living with his brother's wife, so she had him beheaded. In the Gospel I told My apostles how I would be mistreated as well, and even be killed. The worldly are constantly seeking money, fame, and power. The Christians instead are seeking love of God and their neighbor as themselves. Those, who follow Me, I help with their necessities, but they share what they have, and desire to do everything for My greater glory. Those, who kill, cheat, and steal for their own personal gain, are on the path to hell if they do not repent. Do not be surprised then that when you follow My ways, you will be unpopular, criticized, and you may even have to suffer as I suffered at the hands of men. Those, who are faithful to My Word, will have their reward in heaven, despite any abuse that they may suffer for spreading My Gospel."*

Sunday, December 12, 2010: (3ʳᵈ Sunday of Advent,Guadalupe)
At Holy Name after Communion I could see the Star of Bethlehem leading people to Jesus. Jesus said: *"My people, you are getting closer to Christmas as you celebrate the Third Sunday of Advent. Your themes have been 'Stay Awake', 'Repent', and now 'Rejoice'. This celebration of My coming Kingdom is reason for rejoicing, and it is why you see the rose-colored vestments worn today. You have St. John the Baptist preparing the way for My ministry as he calls people forth to change their sinful lives. The vision of the Star of Bethlehem represents My Light that is dispersing the darkness of sin. You are seeing the nights getting longer now. After My birth the nights will grow shorter and the light of day will grow longer. Rejoice in this Advent Season, and be thankful for My coming to save all of you from your sins."*

Later, at St. Theodore's tabernacle I could see a large crowd at a football stadium and the people were being brainwashed with an appearance of the Antichrist as he was being broadcast over the whole world. Jesus said: *"My people, the coming Antichrist will use your large football stadiums to talk to thousands of people at once how he wants to have them worship him with his demonic power of suggestion. He will also have his appearance broadcast to all the other nations via satellite TV. This is how he will spread his influence all over the world. Once he takes power, My people will need to be at their refuges of protection. Do not look at his eyes or listen to his voice. After the Warning, this is why you need to put your TVs and computers out of your homes so he cannot control your minds. Beware of mind control techniques being used on large groups of people wherever they are meeting."*

Monday, December 13, 2010: (St. Lucy)
Later, at Holy Name after Communion I saw a star at first, and then a large spindle of twine representing the length of a person's lifetime. Jesus said: *"My people, when you first start out in life, the length of your life is not a concern. As you get into your 60s, then you start planning more seriously in the event that you could die at any time. You also could die when you are younger, but you really are more concerned once you start collecting Social Security. Your life is full of opportunities to help people, and even more so once you are retired. If you do not have another mission, you can take a small job just to keep busy. Try and make the best use of your time, especially while you are healthy. You can help your family, friends, or spend more time in prayer. You have been busy most of your life, so you will find other things to do once you retire from working. In all of your activities at any age, you need to keep focused on Me as the center of your life. However many years that you are given, keep doing all that you can for My glory."*

Later, at our house praying with the Adoration DVD I could see a large circling saw cut a large piece of ice in two. Jesus said: *"My people, you are experiencing some freezing weather along with some lake effect snow. This saw over the ice in the vision is an idea of the cutting cold weather that is affecting your airplane flights and other vehicle movement in these storms. I have warned you before of how vulnerable you are in the cold winter weather. Imagine if you lost your electricity, how important it would be to have a backup source of heat and light.*

This is why I have asked you to store one year's supply of food, and a winter's supply of wood and kerosene along with the needed heaters. When the one world people want to take you over, you could see how they could control people through their needs for food and fuel. At My refuges My angels will supply your food and shelter needs, so trust in My protection. Even at the refuges, everyone will have their own job to do, as you will be busy in providing for your survival. Pray more that you will guard your soul for its needs of being pure than any needs of the body."

Tuesday, December 14, 2010: (St. John of the Cross)
At Holy Name after Communion I could see an airplane struggling to take off in a snowy storm. Jesus said: *"My people, in your snow and cold many airplane flights were cancelled. Even with all of your sophisticated electronic devices, the weather can humble all of man's plans. There is just so much that man can control, but My creation is too awesome to overcome. Snow and ice storms give a reality lesson to My people whenever you are feeling high and mighty. The rich one world people think that they can control humanity, but they are sadly mistaken. I am still in control, and I will allow the Antichrist a brief reign before I will vanquish all the evil ones into hell in My justice. Just when you think it is hopeless to carry on, I will intervene and set all things to My way as creation first started. Rejoice in My Christmas Season, but you will rejoice even more when I come on the clouds in victory."*

Later, at Holy Cross after Communion I could see some wheat moving around with the wind. Jesus said: *"My people, the wheat is harvested and ground to make flour for bread. It is the unleavened bread that the priest consecrates with the wine into My Body and Blood. Those, who eat My Body and drink My Blood worthily, will have eternal life. My Eucharist is real food for your soul, as you are partaking in My Real Presence that allows you to be My tabernacle until the Host is consumed. Holy Communion gives you the spiritual strength to heal the wounds of your sins, and make you strong against temptations to sin. Be thankful that I give Myself to you at every Mass. St. John of the Cross shows you how important it is to take up your own cross and follow Me in your life's actions. When you carry the cross, you are bearing the burdens of everyday life. Be true to Me and trust in Me that by suffering your cross with Me, you can gain eternal salvation."*

Wednesday, December 15, 2010:

At Holy Name after Communion I could take a close look at nature and its animals among the snow and cold. Jesus said: *"My people, when St. John the Baptist's disciples were asking if I was the Messiah, I gave witness to him of the healing of the blind, the deaf, the lame, and even the dead being raised. These were the prophecies given of when the Redeemer would come, so St. John would recognize these signs. Even in today's world you are still seeing conversions to the faith, and some healings are seen, as well as some exorcisms. My gifts are shared with those who believe, and those that I have given special missions. These miracles are signs for the unbelievers and confirmations to those who serve Me. Most healings of the body are combined with healings of the soul. Many are healed who believe that I can heal them. The most important healing is in saving souls from hell. That is why My evangelists are doing the best service to people that can be done for them. Believe in My Good News, and you will have rest and peace in your soul."*

Later, at St. Theodore's Adoration I could see another snow storm developing. Jesus said: *"My people, your snowfall from lake effect squalls has been heavy already, and it will continue for some time during your winter season. It is one thing to deal with snow storms, but you may also have to deal with another flu season. Your seasonal flu viruses tend to spread when the weather is cold. During the summer these viruses die off before they can infect someone. I have warned you that the one world people will use pandemic viruses in order to reduce the population. Since these viruses survive better in the cold, then they would most likely spread such viruses in the winter by using chemtrails. I will warn you when it is the right time to leave for My refuges. If you come to My refuges soon enough, you will be healed of all sicknesses by looking on My luminous cross or by drinking the spring water. By being at My refuges, the evil ones will not be able to capture you or be able to put microchips in your body. Rejoice that I will protect you and feed you what you need to survive. You will also have My angels feed you My daily Eucharist, and with priests present, you could have Confession of your sins. I will be healing your body and your soul just as I healed the whole body when I was among My people."*

Thursday, December 16, 2010:

At Holy Name after Communion I could see an old junk yard where people had discarded their used items. Jesus said: *"My people, in your society that is always interested in having something new, you have created a second market of used computers and used cars. As these things are passed down, eventually they become so out of date that your used things are thrown into a junk pile. Some people even make a market in old parts as replacements that are cheaper than new parts. In your spiritual life you also are dealing with old sinful habits that you find hard to discard. You also need to be wary of the devil's tricks in calling things 'new' when they are really old. You have a 'New Age' movement which is nothing new because it is nothing more than pagan idol worship dressed up with a 'new' name. It is man's curiosity in these old sins that has attracted him to 'new' sins of old ways. Worship only Me at all times, and you will not be confused or distracted by the devil's tricks."*

Later, at the Eternal Father prayer group at Holy Name Adoration I could see microscopic bar codes being placed in embryos and chips being placed in babies. Jesus said: *"My people, man's fascination with identifying people by placing chips in people should be avoided at all costs to avoid misuse of mind control techniques. Your latest means of bar coding embryos and chipping babies is another tactic by the one world people to control all babies at birth. Those, who have chips in their body, could be controlled by voices from these chips. Do not take any chips in your bodies, even if the evil ones threaten to kill you. This is why you need to come to My refuges so these evil ones cannot put chips into your body."*

I could see continuing riots in Greece because the government was forcing austerity measures on its people to balance their budgets and lower their national debt. Jesus said: *"My people, I have shown you these riots in Greece because America will also have to employ austerity measures when those holding your Treasury Notes demand it. In Greece salaries and pensions are being reduced and the retirement age is being raised. America cannot keep overspending and reducing taxes because your debt is ballooning beyond your ability to finance it. Just as your states are struggling with their debts, both your Federal and state governments will need to balance their budgets or face fiscal bankruptcy. Pray that you work on your debts before they become too large to service."*

I could see our servicemen and women dying in Afghanistan and our war budgets ruining our economy. Jesus said: *"My people, your war in Afghanistan needs to come to an end because you cannot afford the human losses nor the debts they are costing. This war has dragged on for many years without any benefits to show that it is necessary to continue. Terrorists can hide anywhere and rooting out a few hideouts at your current cost cannot be justified. Work to have peace in this area because this war only gives profits to the rich."*

I could see nuclear bomb making going on in Iran and North Korea. Jesus said: *"My people, you are seeing an ongoing proliferation of nuclear weapons in countries advocating war and terrorism. This is why any agreements to lessen your defense does not make sense against rogue states with atomic weapons. A proper defense can be justified, but large weapons budgets could be better spent on helping the poor. Your spending priorities need to be further studied for cuts, and you may need to raise taxes to balance your budget. Spending more stimulus funds has not really given you any more jobs."*

I could see the rich become richer as the bankers and corporations are sitting on all of their profits. Jesus said: *"My people, your corporations and banks have been bailed out with stimulus and bailout money from the taxpayers. As a result, both corporations and banks are making billions of dollars, but jobs are not being funded very much and bank interest for savers is practically non-existent. The intent seems to be to send people's money into stocks so the rich can steal it again with another stock crash. This total control of money is what the one world people want so they can keep your people poor, and keep you under their control. Pray that My justice will come quickly on the evil ones who are greedy for power and riches."*

I could see the Warning and the refuges as an intervention that Jesus will bring to protect His people during the tribulation. Jesus said: *"My people, the Warning is needed to wake up sinners to see how much they need My help to have contrition for their sins, and work to convert their lives to My way of life in order to gain heaven. My intervention in protecting My faithful remnant at My refuges gives hope to all of My people who desire to follow Me instead of the Antichrist. It is My angel protection that will shield My people from the evil ones who are trying to kill you. Be grateful for My intervention against all the evil ones of the coming tribulation."*

I could see a Nativity scene being displayed in public. Jesus said: *"My people, some of My faithful are brave enough to have Nativity scenes as their house decorations outside for Christmas. This is a statement of your belief in why I came on the earth to save mankind from their sins. Rejoice in celebrating this Christmas Season with gifts to each other, but share your gifts as well with the poor who have next to nothing. Help your local food shelves with donations to supply people with food. Give your gifts of prayers as well to help souls come closer in loving Me. By sharing your treasure and evangelization efforts, you will store up treasure for yourselves in heaven."*

Friday, December 17, 2010:
At St. John the Evangelist after Communion I could see the eyes of the Antichrist, and at first they were brown. Then a demon took possession of him and his eyes turned black. Jesus said: *"My people, you are seeing a transformation of the Antichrist from a demon-controlled human into a demon-possessed human. In the vision you are seeing his eyes change from brown into black once the demon entered him. This will take place once he comes into power. This is another reason not to look at the Antichrist's eyes, and to get rid of your TVs and computers after the Warning so you do not see him or hear his voice. This demon possession of the Antichrist is to mock My Incarnation as a man which you are celebrating at My birth. This is why you are to avoid the Antichrist because he will have demonic powers to try and force you to worship him. You will need My protection and that of your guardian angel to bring you to My refuges where you will be protected from this demonic power, and your spiritual and physical needs will be provided for."*

Later, at St. Theodore's tabernacle I could see a hill with a Christmas tree farm on it. I then saw how people routinely put up a Christmas tree and decorate it. Jesus said: *"My people, you read the Scriptures about the events that led up to My birth in Bethlehem. Having a Nativity scene among your Christmas decorations should be essential to celebrating My birth on Christmas. Yet, you have many other traditions about Christmas. St. Nicholas truly did share gifts with the poor, but the reindeer and elves have been more of a story than reality. Every year you put up Christmas trees, but how much do you know of this tradition and where it came from. My Star of Bethlehem is a miracle that led the Wise Men to see Me. This is in Scripture, but many scientists are baffled about how this could happen. Everything in Scripture that prophesied about Me had to be fulfilled. Rejoice that I came on the earth as a man so I could redeem all of mankind by My sacrificial death on the cross."*

Saturday, December 18, 2010:
At St. John the Evangelist after Communion I could see a gold tabernacle from a distance. Jesus said: *"My people, during the Christmas Season you do a lot of shopping to share gifts on Christmas. You can think of the Magi who brought Me gifts of gold, frankincense, and myrrh, befitting a king. As you see the gold tabernacle in the vision, you can think of how you bring Me gifts of your prayers and good deeds, but I give you the gift of Myself every time that you receive Me in Holy Communion. In this way we are also sharing gifts with each other, but more in a spiritual way than in material things. Rejoice in this season of Advent as you share your good will with your relatives and friends, in addition to your physical gifts. When you pray with each other, you are asking Me to share in your joy of worshiping Me as the infant in the crib."*

Later, at Noctural Adoration at Holy Name I could see trucks traveling through a snow storm. Jesus said: *"My people, you are seeing unusually cold and snowy weather, and increasing costs for your fuel in gasoline. There has been an increase in world demand for oil and the value of your dollar has also been dropping. Your government has been spending much more money than it is collecting in taxes, and soon your economy will have to survive without any more stimulus giveaways. As I showed you these trucks, think if they have problems delivering your food and gas to your stores. The drivers are also dealing with higher fuel costs and poor weather. This is another reason to have some extra food and fuel available in case you may face some shortages caused by missed truck deliveries. It is one thing to help poor people with gifts of food, but imagine when many people do not have enough food to eat or fuel for their cars. Many are having hard economic times with fewer jobs or less paying jobs. They do not have many reserves to get through continuing money shortages. Pray that people help each other with their needs, before people get desperate to steal what they need."*

Sunday, December 19, 2010: (4th Sunday of Advent)

At Holy Name after Communion I could see Our Blessed Mother come in an all white dress with her arms outstretched. Our Lady said: *"My dear children, my human spouse was St. Joseph and he was a caring man on earth who took care of me and my Son, Jesus. Even though the evangelists did not record his words, they did record his actions which were very loving in taking me into his home. When I accepted being the Mother of my Savior, I knew that I may be subjected to criticism from the society. But St. Joseph listened to the angel and understood God's plan for Jesus. He also led us to Egypt and back to avoid Herod's attempt to kill my Son. Pray to St. Joseph because he is a model father of my Holy Family. All fathers should see his concern and care for his family, and model their lives after his love for his family. Despite all of life's trials, fathers need to be true to their wives in helping them, and the children in their support. Part of America's moral breakdown comes from the fathers who have left their families in divorce and separation."*

Monday, December 20, 2010:

At Holy Name after Communion I could see a special chapel where the Blessed Mother was met by the Archangel Ga-briel at the Annunciation. Jesus said: *"My people, My Blessed Mother had been prepared for many years to be the sinless virgin who would bring Me into the world. Truly she was 'Blessed' among all women to fulfill this task for all humanity to carry Me in her womb for nine months. My Blessed Mother always did My Will, and this question of St. Gabriel was her fitting time to give her fiat 'yes' to be My mother through the overshadowing by the Holy Spirit. This was the first human step of My redemption of mankind when I became impregnated in My Blessed Mother. This is why My Blessed Mother was an integral part in man's redemption through My Incarnation as a man to later die for mankind's sins. You are about to celebrate My birth at Christmas, but many preparations had to occur before this event could take place. Give thanks to Me and to all of those who were a part of My plan of salvation for mankind."*

Later, at St. Theodore's tabernacle I could see a fife and drum parade in revolutionary times. Jesus said: *"My people, your freedoms in America are being lost every day. All of your remaining freedoms will need defending to keep them from being taken away. Even with your change in the Congress, many good laws may not get passed over your President's veto. You will see increasing regulation coming from the Executive branch that is taking powers away from your Congress and your states. Once your freedoms are taken away as with the North American Union, then My faithful will need to go to My refuges for protection from being killed by the one world people. Enjoy the few freedoms that you have now, because you will see more and more dictatorial power forced on your people. Pray that most of you can get to My refuges before being martyred."*

Tuesday, December 21, 2010: (St. Canisius)

At Holy Name after Communion I could look around a round corner as related to what is coming tomorrow. Jesus said: *"My people, many people are always worrying about what will happen tomorrow, which is why you are looking around the corner in the vision. You can do what is prudent for everyday planning for tomorrow, but you cannot live your life in tomorrow. You can only live today, and the troubles of today are enough for your concern. It is the present where you act out your plans, and even at times you have to change your daily plans because of changed circumstances. Focus on doing everything for My greater glory, instead of seeking glory for your own deeds. Also, do not live in the past either, because you need to have faith in Me to lead you on a better path learning from your mistakes. By living in the present, you will be able to focus all of your energy on your work at hand without worrying about tomorrow or yesterday."*

Later, at St. Theodore's tabernacle I could see a communications line of fiber optics with a tear in the line to see all the wires packed together. Jesus said: *"My people, I have mentioned before how vulnerable you are if your electricity is cut off. You are also vulnerable to a communications break down as well. You have become so used to making bank transactions over the internet for individuals and for businesses. You also transmit data and voice messages over your phone and cell phone. Depending on the electric source for the phone lines, land lines have their own electric source, but cell phones would not work without electricity. You can realize how everything would come to a halt without such communications. In the spiritual world our lines of communication are always open, even after your death. The only problem could come if a person does not want to talk to Me in any form of prayer. I am always knocking on the door of your heart and soul, and you have to open the door from the inside in order to have a working love relationship with Me. So work with Me on your prayers. You need an open mind, heart, and soul to accomplish your mission on earth. The point of My message on communications is that you have to keep the line open so we can have a two-way conversation. Give thanks to Me for enabling you to do all that you are accomplishing."*

Wednesday, December 22, 2010:

At St. John the Evangelist after Communion I could see the cave in Bethlehem and at first there was the empty creche. Then the Light of the Star shown down on the baby Jesus in the crib. Jesus said: *"My people, in today's Gospel you are reading My Blessed Mother's Magnificat that is read every night in the Liturgy of the Hours. She is a model to follow because she lived in My Divine Will, and she was sinless her whole life because of her love for Me. She was blessed to be My mother, but she was humble, followed My Will, and reached out to help others as she helped Elizabeth in her late pregnancy. She was a good teacher in My younger years, and she was a beacon of faith for My apostles. Give thanks and glory to God that you have such a loving spiritual mother who watches out for all of her children."*

Later, at St. Theodore's Adoration I could see a severe ice storm that lasted several days. Jesus said: *"My people, your winter has just started and you are already seeing high snowfalls in some areas, and floods in California. Even tonight you are having a small amount of freezing rain. Some have had power outages from heavy snow, but you know how devastating ice storms are for power outages. Pray that you do not suffer such a storm this winter. Whenever you see freezing rain, it is a sign to you to check that you have some extra food, alternate fuel for heat, and lamp oil for lights. Having some windup flashlights that work would also be good to have on hand for seeing at night. In some Northern states you have been without power for a few weeks in the past years, so you know how difficult it is to keep warm without electricity. You also may want to test your alternate heaters to make sure that they are in working order. I mentioned these preparations before, but when you have a near miss ice storm, you get a reality check on something that could easily happen."*

Thursday, December 23, 2010:

At Holy Name after Communion I could see people looking down on the infant Jesus, and there was someone holding a lantern overhead for light. Jesus said: *"My people, there were many events that had to be fulfilled for My plan of salvation to be carried out. One miraculous event was the birth of St. John the Baptist to his parents Elizabeth and Zachariah who were advanced in years, for everything is possible for Me. Zachariah was struck deaf and dumb for not believing St. Gabriel's message that he would have a son. At the birth of St. John, Zachariah gave a beautiful canticle that is read in the morning for the Liturgy of the Hours. St. John was prepared as My messenger in the desert who would herald My coming and prepare the people with repentance. As you are about to celebrate another Christmas, you can see how all the pieces of salvation history were orchestrated and brought together so all souls could be redeemed by My sacrifice."*

Later, at the Eternal Father prayer group at Holy Name Adoration I could see many Nativity scenes at various churches. Jesus said: *"My people, as you are about to celebrate Christmas, there is much preparation at each church to give honor to My birth. This year your church's Nativity scene is especially beautiful with your different statues. Many of your people will be grateful for these beautiful decorations. Christmas is a solemn feast day in My Church, and it is one of the major highlights in your Church Year. As you celebrate in giving your gifts to each other, remember to say your decade of the rosary before you open your gifts."*

I could see in a house where a Christmas tree had been placed. Then a large crack appeared in the floor from an earthquake and the Christmas tree fell through the floor. Jesus said: *"My people, even as you celebrate My feast of Christmas, remember in your prayers to pray especially for those families who have lost their homes to various natural disasters or terrorist actions. Some terrorists plan their attacks around Christian holy days as a defiance against any belief in My coming as the Son of Man. They believe that I was only a prophet, and not God incarnate as a man. My coming to earth as a man had an exact reason, to bring salvation to all of mankind by My death on the cross. Defend My Incarnation as a man to witness to the world that God truly has visited His people."*

I could see the light of the angels in the cave at the moment that Jesus was born. Jesus said: *"My people, the angels sang My song of glory for the shepherds, and they led the shepherds to My crib at Bethlehem. Rejoice in their singing: 'Glory to God in the highest and on earth peace among men of good will.' The angels brought their light to My crib. Wherever you see Me, as in My Blessed Sacrament, My angels are around Me singing My songs of praise as they do in heaven. If you were to see Me in heaven, you could hear all the choirs of angels singing My constant praises."*

I could see many spotlights in Hollywood as they displayed their new movies. There was only one spotlight in Bethlehem and that came from the Star that led the Magi to Bethlehem. Jesus said: *"My people, in My day there were not many ways to draw attention to a great event as My birth. So I used natural means to display notice for a supernatural event when I was born as a man into your world in the history of time. You have recorded history of My time on earth as you measure your years by before and after My birth. There are some atheists that want to do away with the meanings of B.C. and A.D. See that I watch over My people, and I love you so much that I died for each one of you."*

I could still see people honoring the old Temple at the Wailing Wall in Jerusalem. Jesus said: *"My people, there is a great richness in the promise of a Redeemer who would come to My Jewish people. This vision of the Wailing Wall represents the remnants of the old Temple. I have built My Church on a new rock in My apostles, and on the kingdom that I brought into the world. I have come to save all peoples of all nations, and not just the Jewish people. When St. Paul reached out to the Gentiles, you could see the true universality of My Word that I have brought to all of mankind, even if some do not believe in Me."*

I could see some new churches being built, while other churches are being closed. Jesus said: *"My people, you are seeing some areas expanding My churches, but there are more churches being closed. Where the faith is strong, there are plenty of priestly vocations and whole families are coming every Sunday to Mass. Where the faith is weak, your attendance at Mass is falling and there are priest shortages. My religious leaders need to do their job in building up the faithful numbers."*

I could see families and friends coming together to share their joy and gifts with each other on Christmas. Jesus said: *"My people, if you truly want to come and share your gifts with Me on Christmas, then make an effort to come to Mass on Christmas Day or the vigil so you can be with Me in My Eucharist. My sacramental Presence reaches out to all of you so you can share in the graces of My Eucharist. Christmas is one of My great feast days, so you should make an effort to come out to greet Me and give Me praise and glory in your singing. Pray for all of your family and friends that you could be an inspiration in leading them to Me in heaven. Saving souls should be your most important vocation in life."*

Friday, December 24, 2010:

At St. John the Evangelist after Communion I could see travelers coming from a distance for the census as Joseph and Mary had to travel to Bethlehem. Jesus said: *"My people, I was fortunate to find a place to stay in a cave for the animals. Today, many families travel great distances to be with each other on Christmas Day. You usually have a big meal and then share your gifts around the Christmas tree. Only this year you will be praying a decade of the rosary before opening your gifts. Remember this moment with your pictures as you pray for your family members to save their souls. You have seen in the Scriptures how the shepherds and the Magi traveled a great distance to see the new born King. Even today, you would travel a distance to receive Me at a Mass. In some areas of the South you had to travel hundreds of miles to find a Catholic Church. In the coming tribulation you also will find it difficult to have a priest for a Mass. By the grace of My angels you will have daily Communion, even if you do not have a Mass. Rejoice while you still have your churches for daily Mass, because a time is coming when they will be closed by the evil ones."*

(Vigil Mass) At Holy Name after Communion I could see out into the universe as Our Lord and Master took on human flesh to become one of us as a man. Jesus said: *"My people, in this vision you know that I am the Second Person of the Blessed Trinity. Yet, with all of My power in the universe, I was able to take on a human nature and I still remained God and Divine at the same time. This Incarnation into a human is a mystery that is hard for man to comprehend. Still, becoming a man was part of My means to redeem all of mankind. Many prophecies were given of My coming, but some people had different expectations of Me coming as a powerful king to free the Jews from the Romans. Many had difficulty in accepting My Gospel of love because it meant changing from a life of greed and pleasure. Even the people of today have the same difficulty because man's desires and wants have not changed over the years. The real understanding comes when each of you discover that you have a spiritual life in your soul that can only be satisfied with My peace. Follow your spiritual desires to be with Me more than any worldly desires of the body."*

Saturday, December 25, 2010: (Christmas Day)
At Holy Name after Communion I could see the infant Jesus in the manger which is a sign to all of us. Jesus said: *"My people, I am your Lord and God at any age, even as an infant. You can pray to Me as Santo Nino, a twelve-year-old boy, or as a grown adult because I am the same Jesus. I could have come with more glorious power, but I came as an innocent baby, born to a poor family. I chose a humble beginning with very little of My younger life that was recorded in the Scriptures. It was My teaching ministry and My Passion and death that you know the most about because that was My mission on earth to redeem all of you. You all are born as innocent children, and it is what you do with your life that you will be held accountable for. I have given you My life as a model to follow as well as My Blessed Mother. We were without sin, but you can still strive for perfection in this life. Call on Me to help you every day to follow My laws and share your gifts with everyone."*

Sunday, December 26, 2010: (Holy Family Sunday)
At Holy Name after Communion I could see a fishing reel. Jesus said: *"My people, this Sunday is dedicated to My Holy Family, but it is also meant for all families. Just as I called fisherman to be My apostles, I am always searching for souls to pull them into My love. The family is based on love and it is beautiful. A man and woman are joined in marriage with the sacrament of Matrimony. It is love that brought them together for a life long commitment. Just as it is out of love that I have created everything, so it is out of love that children are brought into the world. It is in this family setting of loving parents that the children are raised up to adults. This is why fornication, adultery, and divorce are destroying family life in the way that I meant it to be among you. Marriage is a responsibility in faith as well as living according to My laws. Living together does not have the same commitment in neither faith nor bringing up children. When your society is more concerned with pleasure*

and materialism instead of living in loving marriages, then you can see
the downfall coming in your country. Pray for all married people and
that your children see the need to avoid living together in sin."

Later, at St. Theodore's tabernacle I could see a stage of life with
burning flames across the front of the stage and a circling piece of round
glass like a clock. Jesus said: *"My people, all of the signs and symbols*

in the vision are another description of the coming Warning. The stage of life is where you perform your daily actions, both good and bad. The flames represent the souls of life who are each accountable in their life review. The circling glass clock means that the time of the Warning is getting close. Your life review will focus on your unforgiven sins, so your best preparation is to go to frequent Confession at least monthly. The Warning will be an opportunity for even the worst sinner to have a second chance at changing their lifestyle. This will be a spiritual wake-up call also for all the lukewarm souls who could be lost if they do not change their lazy ways. Your judgment will show you where you are headed if you continue on your present path. Returning to your body will give you a second chance to be saved which is more than those who die without this opportunity. Keep focused on Me as your love that you would want to be with. By accepting Me as Master of your life and seeking the forgiveness of your sins, you could receive eternal life in heaven."

Monday, December 27, 2010: (St. John the Evangelist)
At Holy Name after Communion I could see a place in Ephesus, Turkey where there was a sign that named St. John's burial place. Jesus said: *"My people, St. John is the one apostle who loved Me most as His Master. He was the only apostle not to be martyred, and he took care of My Blessed Mother in her later years. He wrote his Gospel later with a heavy emphasis on My Resurrection, as he saw the empty tomb in today's Gospel. He also wrote some letters and the Book of Revelation on Patmos. His writings are words of hope and encouragement for My faithful. His words on eating My Body and drinking My Blood that would give eternal life are very direct and profound. His words about the end times are very connected to My son's mission of preparation. Continue to proclaim My promises, and keep leading My people to My refuges of protection. Know that in the end I will defeat the evil ones and bring about My Era of Peace."*

Later, at Theodore's tabernacle I could see some lava and smoke coming from many volcanoes that were linked to an increase in earthquakes. Jesus said: *"My people, with a steady number of volcanic explosions, you have seen a lot of smoke and particles get placed in the upper atmosphere. With a sufficient amount of clouds and dust, there could be a reduced amount of sunlight that could have a cooling effect on the earth's temperature. Unless there is an increase in sunspot activity, there may be more global cooling than global warming.* Just when *scientists think global trends are going in one direction, then natural occurrences create an equilibrium with no net change. The bigger events will be going on with an increase in evil more than any natural disasters. Pray that My faithful will be ready to go to My refuges before more of My faithful are martyred."*

Tuesday, December 28, 2010: (Holy Innocents)

At St. John the Evangelist after Communion I could see Moses celebrating the Passover meal as there were many parallels with Jesus. Jesus said: *"My people, you saw Moses in the vision today as the parallels with Me are many. We were both threatened with death in our infancies. Moses was protected from death by the Pharaoh's daughter, and I was taken to Egypt with My parents so Herod could not kill Me. Herod killed all the boys up to two years old in Bethlehem, which is the reason for today's feast honoring these holy, innocent babies. Even today many innocent babies are still being killed by abortion. Moses had a mission to save his people from the Egyptians as he brought them to the Promised Land. I had a mission to save all of humanity from their sins by My death on the cross. Moses celebrated the Passover meal with unleavened bread and the wine. At the Last Supper I also celebrated the Passover meal, but I consecrated the bread and wine into My very Body and Blood. This is a new spiritual manna that gives eternal life at every Mass. When Moses was in the desert, there was miraculous food and water that were multiplied. During My ministry I performed many miracles as well in multiplying the bread and fish for the multitudes of people on two occasions. Moses raised up the bronze serpent to heal the people from their snake bites. I was raised up on a cross and many were healed by the sacrifice of My Blood. There are many such parallels of the Old Testament accounts with the New Testament. As you read the Scripture accounts, you can learn how to be a good Christian by loving Me and your neighbor as yourself."*

Later, at St. Theodore's Adoration I could see a large church in the city and on the door there was a foreclosure sign. Jesus said: *"My people, keeping the city churches open has become a financial problem for the pastors of these churches. Every church has expenses to keep operating: for mortgages, heating, lighting, and paying the staff.*

Some Catholics still think that they can just put a few dollars in the basket and the church will keep running. All church expenses have to be covered by the donations of those who attend. In the city the people may be hard pressed to donate what is needed to keep the church open. Not only are your city churches dealing with poor attendance, but the people cannot afford to pay much. Without some big supporters, these churches will be closing by the hundreds. This is the current problem, but in the future the persecution will close all churches as in Russia at one time. My faithful will soon need to have Mass and prayer groups in the homes. This is why I have asked you to have Mass needs in the home and prepare your priests for when they will have to flee or come to your homes. As the religious persecution gets worse, you will be forced to come to My refuges of protection. Call on My help and I will provide for all of your needs at My refuges."

Wednesday, December 29, 2010: (St. Thomas Becket)
At Holy Name after Communion I could see a cave as in the catacombs. Jesus said: *"My people, in days past when My faithful were being martyred for their faith, some hid in caves as the catacombs around Rome. In other places in the Bible, Elijah and other prophets hid in caves to avoid being killed by those who did not like their message. My son, your message of preparation in the end times is also a difficult message that many do not want to hear. As the persecution gets worse leading up to the Antichrist, your life and others will also be at risk for martyrdom. A time will come when you will be called into hiding at My refuges. I want all of My faithful to never deny their love for Me, even if it means that your life may be endangered. Better to die a martyr's death than live your life in denial of your faith. Many people put their life on the line as soldiers or policemen. If you could risk death for a good cause, how much more should you be willing to die for your faith in Me. Dying as a martyr may be a difficult decision, but I will give all of My faithful the strength to endure this test if it is required of them in the coming tribulation."*

Later, at St. Theodore's Adoration I could see an empty throne where the Antichrist will take control of the world. Jesus said: *"My people, this vision of an empty throne is a sign that the Antichrist will be coming into power in a short time. I have given you messages before that the one world people are forming unions on every continent to focus power on the unions and away from any people who are patriotic to their country. Once they have formed these unions, as the European Union and the North American Union, then the one world people will give control of these unions over to the Antichrist who will be allowed to control the world. His seat of power will be set up in the European Union and the Antichrist will have a reign of power over less than 3 ½ years. This will begin a reign of evil that you have never seen before. Once the Antichrist declares himself, My faithful will need to seek My protection at My refuges. Refuse to take any chip in the body, and refuse to worship him. Do not look at his eyes or listen to his voice. By following My direction you will have angels at My refuges who will protect you from any evil demons, or virus diseases. Trust in Me and I will come to defeat the evil ones and bring about My Era of Peace."*

Thursday, December 30, 2010:

At St. John the Evangelist after Communion I could see a man in prison with shackles and chains. Jesus said: *"My people, you have read of St. John the Baptist in chains, and also St. Peter and St. Paul. Many of My disciples and apostles were captured in prison with chains, and later they were martyred for their faith. This religious persecution is about to be repeated in the coming tribulation. You will again see some of My people shackled on trains and delivered to the current death camps for execution. This is why I am preparing refuges with people that I have inspired, so My faithful will have places to go in order to avoid being captured by the one world people. Some will be martyred for their faith, but I will lessen the pain to allow them to endure it. These martyrs will become instant saints in heaven. For those, who come to My refuges, they will be protected from harm by My angels, and I will provide for their needs during the reign of the Antichrist. Have no fear, for I will give you My peace in all of this struggle. After the Antichrist's time, I will come with My victory over all the evil ones, and I will establish My Era of Peace."*

Later, at the Eternal Father prayer group at Holy Name Adoration I could see a spinning globe with a football field in the background. Jesus said: *"My people, this spinning globe is a sign of how I will speed up the earth on its axis so the time of the tribulation will be shortened for the sake of the elect. The football field represents the time from September to February when the Warning will most likely occur. My people can* prepare themselves with prayer and Confession of their unforgiven sins. The Warning will be your sign of the events that will lead up to the coming of the Antichrist into power."

I could see hundreds of 72-hour candles that were blessed for use in the Three Days of Darkness. Jesus said: *"My people, at the end of the tribulation I will bring My Comet of Chastisement to enable My victory over all of the evil ones. As the comet strikes the earth, many volcanoes will erupt, and the ash will block out the sun creating the Three Days of Darkness. In the vision you are seeing 72-hour blessed candles that will give the only light during this darkness. Remember to take such a candle with you in your backpacks on your way to My refuges."*

I could look at the roof of a house that was at a refuge. Jesus said: *"My people, I have asked My refuge builders to have one building dedicated for sleeping quarters for My faithful. This is why you are looking at the roof of such a building, as I will multiply such buildings as needed. Those, who are preparing their refuges, need to have some food, fuel, and water so I could multiply these things that people need for their survival."*

I could see some door handles, but there were no locks on the doors. Jesus said: *"My people, all of My faithful that come to My refuges know and follow My Commandments. Among all the buildings that will house My faithful, you will all be on the honor system with no stealing accepted. You will all be in loving communities that will not require locks as you do now in the world where there are thieves. Just as you trust in Me, so you will have to trust each other because everything belongs to Me, and I share it with all of you. By helping each other to survive by using your own talents, everyone will have what they need. Be loving of each other as you pray to Me. You are all one family with Me as I protect you from the evil ones."*

I could see a picture of our freedom bell in Philadelphia. Jesus said: *"My people, freedoms are granted to everyone from My authority. When your leaders or Congress take away your freedoms, they are not serving the common good because they are serving only themselves. Various forms of government have been time tested, but unless you work to preserve your freedoms, others will take control over you. This is why following My laws and keeping your focus on Me is very crucial for any form of government to continue."*

I could see someone building a fence around their property. Jesus said: *"My people, all forms of government need to have a means to defend themselves against outside armies. You may have a good republic democracy, but without a proper defense, other peoples could destroy you. Defending one's country is acceptable, but using military might to control your neighbors is an abuse of your power. America has defended others from dictatorial leaders who wanted to control the world. America does not have the right to change other countries for your own gain. Fight to keep peace in the world so everyone will have the same freedoms."*

I could see a New Year starting, but there was much chaos and confusion over where our leaders will take us. Jesus said: *"My people, you have a new Congress running your government, and there will be some hard decisions that need to be made in order to keep America from collapsing. Pray that your leaders will follow My model of love instead of following their own greed. America's deficits and overspending need to be reined in or you will be headed for bankruptcy and collapse of civil order. Balancing budgets, even if austerity budgets are required, will cause some conflicts when people do not have their expected entitlements. Compromises will be required for what is best for your country to survive. If there is no change, then you will see the chaos and confusion in the vision that could result. Pray that your leaders make the right decisions for your country to survive."*

Friday, December 31, 2010: (Paul Macaluso's Funeral Mass)
At Holy Spirit Church after Communion I could see a scene of a deli meat counter where Paul visited. Jesus said: *"My people, it is a very sad occasion when parents have to bury their younger son, as Paul. This vision at a deli meat counter was how Paul loved to eat and share with his family. A sudden and unexpected death is also hard on the family who wanted to hear his last words. My Blessed Mother and I met Paul when he died, and he was met also by his deceased relatives. Paul sends his love to all of his family and friends. He is in a peaceful place, but he asks all of you to have Masses said for him. He will be watching out for all of you. Paul was grateful for all the prayers that were said for him, and also for those who were instrumental in allowing him Confession, the last rites, and the scapular. He wanted you all to remember him by visiting his grave from time to time."*

Later, at our home praying with the Adoration DVD I could see actors acting out a movie on the stage of life. Jesus said: *"My people, you have seen movies before, but when you get to know the actors behind the scenes, it adds depth to how these actors can perform. My people are also actors on the stage of life, but you also know the actors in your life and how you fit into their life experiences. Movies are run by a script, but in real life there is no script. You are all asked to be the best that you could be. Each person has their own talents, but I call each of you to use your talents to carry out the mission in life that I have called you to accomplish. You all have to pick up your cross and carry it with Me. Share your suffering with My suffering on the cross. By following My laws of loving Me and your neighbor as yourself, you will gain eternal life with Me in heaven."*

Index

deer meat prepared at refuges (Jesus)	11/3/2010
Defense spending constant wars, blood money (Jesus)	11/4/2010
deficit spending means for US takeover (Jesus)	11/18/2010
deficits, curtail could cause riots (Jesus)	12/2/2010
deficits, overspending cause bankruptcy, inflation (Jesus)	10/7/2010
Division in Church schismatic vs faithful remnant (Jesus)	10/6/2010
Divisions in Church Eastern Rite,Luther,Anglicans (Jesus)	10/6/2010
DVD, new alert for refuges (Jesus)	11/15/2010
DVD, new need St. Therese novena (Jesus)	11/11/2010
DVD, new St. Therese novena (Jesus)	11/15/2010
election opportunity to vote for moral leaders (Jesus)	10/28/2010
election result reduce spending,deficits, +jobs (Jesus)	11/4/2010
electricity shutdown consequences at homes (Jesus)	11/16/2010
electricity stopped one world people control (Jesus)	11/1/2010
EMP attacks store chips deep underground (Jesus)	11/1/2010
EMP weapons devastating to society (Jesus)	11/5/2010
end time preparation backpacks,tents, blankets (Jesus)	10/31/2010
end time readings rarely in homilies (Jesus)	10/21/2010
end times prepare for refuges (Jesus)	11/14/2010
end times prep pure soul, Confession (Jesus)	11/27/2010
entitlements causing state deficits (Jesus)	10/5/2010
entitlements US cannot afford benefits (Jesus)	12/2/2010
Era of Peace joy after Chastisement (Jesus)	10/15/2010
eternal life eat Body, drink Blood (Jesus)	12/2/2010
eternal life repent, ten Commandments (Jesus)	11/4/2010
eternal life promised eating Body, drinking Blood (Jesus)	10/12/2010
Eucharist heals sins, fights temptations (Jesus)	12/14/2010
Evangelists best healing in souls (Jesus)	12/15/2010
evil killers on path to hell (Jesus)	12/11/2010
faith, act of not worthy to come under roof (Jesus)	11/29/2010
family needs support or America will fall (Jesus)	10/26/2010
family of love environment for children (Jesus)	12/26/2010
Federal Reserve adding to debt (Jesus)	11/11/2010
Federal Reserve quantitative easing,dollar down (Jesus)	11/4/2010
financial crisis caused by central bankers (Jesus)	11/6/2010
flowers, late color in creation (Jesus)	10/28/2010
flu shots avoid taking,has viruses (Jesus)	11/3/2010
flu viruses spead more in winter (Jesus)	12/15/2010
food & fuel have extra for outages (Jesus)	11/24/2010
food & fuel shortages stock for power outages (Jesus)	11/18/2010
food & fuel storage weather & money problems (Jesus)	12/18/2010
foreclosed homes banks afraid to lose money (Jesus)	10/7/2010
fornication in America downfall in loss of morals (Jesus)	12/26/2010
freedoms need to be preserved (Jesus)	12/30/2010
fresh water membrane, desalinization (Jesus)	12/7/2010
fresh water need at refuges,survival (Jesus)	12/7/2010
fuels at refuges tractors,cook,heat,light (Jesus)	11/11/2010
garbage at refuges burn, bury, mulch (Jesus)	11/11/2010
gifts to Jesus prayers & good deeds (Jesus)	12/18/2010
global trends nature brings equilibrium (Jesus)	12/27/2010
God's Word, sharing causes division in peoples (Jesus)	10/21/2010
Good News vs world news soul vs. body (Jesus)	11/8/2010
good works can have devil attack (Jesus)	11/11/2010
Gospel & Commandments give witness to save souls (Jesus)	11/23/2010
graces, mercies overflowing to help all souls (Jesus)	11/21/2010
Guadalupe image Our Lady of Americas (Jesus)	12/9/2010
guardian angel mutual love with soul (Jesus)	12/3/2010
HAARP machine control weather in US,Russia (Jesus)	10/18/2010
Halloween costumes do not need evil influences (Jesus)	10/21/2010
Health Plan refuse chips in body (Jesus)	11/15/2010
Health Plan tou use chips in body (Jesus)	11/8/2010
heaters, alternate keep in working order (Jesus)	12/22/2010
heaven seek the higher levels (Jesus)	10/4/2010
heaven or hell follow or reject Jesus (Jesus)	11/17/2010
heaven, be saved follow God's Will & laws (Jesus)	12/2/2010
heaven, higher levels devotions,works,save souls (Jesus)	10/4/2010
hell save souls while still time (Jesus)	12/1/2010
hell, avoid get people to Confession (Jesus)	10/28/2010
heresies inaction will get purgatory (Jesus)	10/25/2010
heretical teaching stand up against (Jesus)	10/25/2010
highways controlled chips, cameras (Jesus)	11/18/2010
Holy days of obligation should be attended (Jesus)	10/28/2010
Holy Grail relics of Jesus' time (Jesus)	12/9/2010
human bodies Temples of Holy Spirit (Jesus)	11/9/2010
humility needed to gain heaven (Jesus)	10/24/2010
Immaculate Conception Mary, Ark of Covenant (Jesus)	12/8/2010
Incarnation of Jesus hard to comprehend (Jesus)	12/24/2010
Indonesian volcano Merapi kills hundreds (Jesus)	11/9/2010
Jesus & Mary, models strive for perfection (Jesus)	12/25/2010
Jesus more powerful than all of the evil ones (Jesus)	11/24/2010
Jesus same at any age as infant,boy, or adult (Jesus)	12/25/2010
Jesus, redeemer on cross conquered sin & death (Jesus)	10/12/2010
jobs not increasing with stimulus & bailouts (Jesus)	12/16/2010
judgment of souls good to heaven,bad to hell (Jesus)	11/17/2010
judgment preparation Confession, do good works (Jesus)	11/22/2010
Kingship of Jesus our Master & Creator (Jesus)	11/23/2010
Lepanto Battle sign of rosary's power (Jesus)	10/7/2010
life's moments in pictures at funerals (Jesus)	12/4/2010
lukewarm Catholics causing low Mass attendance (Jesus)	10/2/2010
lukewarm vs prayer warrior repent, do good works (Jesus)	11/10/2010
lukewarm wake-up mini-judgment in Warning (Jesus)	12/26/2010

manufacturing jobs corporations shipping out (Jesus) 10/5/2010
Mark, my angel personal advice Mark" 10/2/2010
marriage vs pagan living together (Jesus) 11/25/2010
marriage attacked divorce, living together (Jesus) 10/26/2010
marriage polls half live together (Jesus) 11/18/2010
martial law begin purge of Christians (Jesus) 11/30/2010
martial law end of American government (Jesus) 10/4/2010
martial law license to kill religious (Jesus) 12/10/2010
martial law VIPs in underground cities (Jesus) 11/14/2010
martial law, chips time for refuges (Jesus) 11/20/2010
martyrs ease pain, go to heaven (Jesus) 11/22/2010
martyr's choice God's strength to endure (Jesus) 12/29/2010
martyrs for Christ suffered in early persecution (Jesus) 12/30/2010
martyrs for faith better than living in denial (Jesus) 12/29/2010
Mary's apparitions pray the rosary (Mary) 10/7/2010
Masonic control CFR,Bilderbergs,Trilateral Com (Jesus) 11/4/2010
Mass & Adoration core prayer warriors (Jesus) 10/1/2010
Mass translation how received (Jesus) 11/16/2010
Masses, home coming in persecution time (Jesus) 12/3/2010
media control censored news, no content (Jesus) 11/18/2010
Merry Christmas keep focus on Jesus (Jesus) 12/5/2010
messengers messages on refuge prep (Jesus) 10/30/2010
messengers of today use media to save souls (Jesus) 10/5/2010
military defense should not be abused (Jesus) 12/30/2010
mind control remove TVs & computers (Jesus) 12/12/2010
mind control with chips not told by government (Jesus) 11/8/2010
mine accidents safety, fixed violations reduce (Jesus) 10/14/2010
missionaries Jesuits, Redemptorists (Jesus) 10/30/2010
mortal sin, conversion darkness to light of grace (Jesus) 10/17/2010
Moses, Jesus parallels death threats, saving people (Jesus) 12/28/2010
mountains, graces at Moses, apparition sites (Jesus) 12/10/2010
multiplication of food at refuges in end times (Jesus) 12/1/2010
Muslim extremists desire to kill Chrisitans (Jesus) 11/29/2010
National Health ID leads to chip in the body (Jesus) 11/4/2010
Nativity statues new to our church (Jesus) 12/23/2010
nature's beauty reflection of God's love (Jesus) 11/17/2010
nature's disasters can humble mankind (Jesus) 12/14/2010
New Age movement old idol worship (Jesus) 12/16/2010
new Rochester bishop mission, priests, RTL (Jesus) 11/11/2010
North American Union loss of sovereignty rights (Jesus) 11/4/2010
North American Union time for the refuges (Jesus) 12/20/2010
nuclear defense necessary against terrorists (Jesus) 12/16/2010
Obama socialism banks,cars,health industry (Jesus) 10/7/2010
old age thoughts focus on Jesus,plan for heaven (Jesus) 12/13/2010
one world control threaten food & electricity (Jesus) 12/13/2010
one world people directed by Satan (Jesus) 10/21/2010

one world people planning US bankruptcy (Jesus) 11/6/2010
one world people put population to 500 million (Jesus) 10/15/2010
one world people records on everyone (Jesus) 11/15/2010
pandemic virus deadly to flu shot people (Jesus) 11/3/2010
parents responsible for kids' souls (Jesus) 11/19/2010
Paul Macaluso funeral Mass message (Jesus) 12/31/2010
peace & no fear in your souls (Jesus) 11/24/2010
peace over war prayers for (Jesus) 11/11/2010
persecution testing before Era of Peace (Jesus) 10/16/2010
persecution by evil ones threaten to martyr faithful (Jesus)11/22/2010
persecution of Christians to return in tribulation (Jesus) 10/14/2010
persecution, religious forcing Masses in homes (Jesus) 10/8/2010
personal travel to refuges, monstrance (Jesus) 10/16/2010
personal mission connected to St. John (Jesus) 12/27/2010
political dirty tricks to fight Tea Party (Jesus) 10/21/2010
politicians, corrupt censure for money handling (Jesus) 12/2/2010
poor's needs money & food as gifts (Jesus) 12/16/2010
power outage prep food, fuel, oil lamps (Jesus) 12/22/2010
power outages have extra food available (Jesus) 12/6/2010
prayer groups in secret at night (Jesus) 10/14/2010
prayer warriors give will over to Jesus (Jesus) 10/1/2010
prayer warriors use gifts to save souls (Jesus) 10/20/2010
prayer warriors dying replace with young warriors (Jesus) 11/7/2010
prayer, answers to persistent, some 'no' (Jesus) 11/13/2010
prayers on Christmas before opening gifts (Jesus) 12/24/2010
prayers, Adoration love of God (Jesus) 11/28/2010
prayers, Mass lessen time in purgatory (Jesus) 11/2/2010
present, live in not in tomorrow or past (Jesus) 12/21/2010
priests support work with sacraments (Jesus) 12/3/2010
priests should emphasize Confession, Host (Jesus) 11/5/2010
priests to refuges at persecution time (Jesus) 12/9/2010
priests, bishops need to build faith basics (Jesus) 10/2/2010
purgatory most souls suffer this (Jesus) 12/1/2010
purgatory prayers,Mass shorten time (Jesus) 11/7/2010
purgatory, lower no God, suffer flames (Jesus) 11/2/2010
purgatory, upper no presence of God (Jesus) 11/2/2010
Readings at Mass see context in Bible (Jesus) 11/8/2010
Real Presence Host in man as tabernacle (Jesus) 12/14/2010
Real Presence in Host faith, God in Eucharist (Jesus) 11/29/2010
Redeemer in Jesus saves all peoples (Jesus) 12/23/2010
redemption of mankind assisted by Mary (Jesus) 12/20/2010
refuge Adoration 24 hrs. of Real Presence (Jesus) 10/16/2010
refuge buildings multiplied as needed (Jesus) 12/30/2010
refuge caves need Light of Jesus (Jesus) 10/27/2010
refuge life manual labor,prayer,Adoration (Jesus) 11/30/2010
refuge places apparition sites,holy ground,caves (Jesus) 10/14/2010

Prepare for the Great Tribulation and the Era of Peace

refuge places apparition sites,holy ground,caves (Jesus)	10/31/2010
refuge preparations backpacks, lights (Jesus)	11/27/2010
refuge time bankruptcy,virus,chip in body (Jesus)	11/11/2010
refuge time when evil gets worse (Jesus)	10/26/2010
refuges better than underground cities (Jesus)	11/2/2010
refuges have no electricity (Jesus)	11/16/2010
refuges, no locks honor system, no theft (Jesus)	12/30/2010
religion classes challenge any heresies (Jesus)	10/25/2010
religious persecution all churches closed (Jesus)	12/28/2010
religious persecution destruction of,closing churches (Jesus)	12/6/2010
religious persecution from one world people (Jesus)	11/30/2010
religious persecution in tribulation, martyrs again (Jesus)	12/30/2010
responsibility more you have,more expected (Jesus)	10/20/2010
revelation on mountains love, messages of comfort (Jesus)	12/10/2010
riots, false flag could cause martial law (Jesus)	12/10/2010
Roman census plan for Jesus at Bethlehem (Jesus)	12/9/2010
roofs with snow clear,avoid icicles,leaks (Jesus)	12/7/2010
Rosario Proia funeral message (Jesus)	11/17/2010
rosary weapon against evil (Jesus)	10/7/2010
sacraments protection from temptations (Jesus)	10/23/2010
Santo Nino novena prayers at Christmas (Jesus)	12/9/2010
satellites, orbit decay fall to earth as meteors (Jesus)	12/9/2010
sermon for 30 minutes better than 10 min homily (Jesus)	10/2/2010
sermon on faith daily prayers, Adoration (Jesus)	11/28/2010
sexual sins, mortal fornication, birth control (Jesus)	11/26/2010
signs of Jesus' coming conversions,healings,exorcism (Jesus)	12/15/2010
signs of Jesus' coming evil worse, lukewarm faith (Jesus)	10/11/2010
sinful behavior do not follow the crowd (Jesus)	10/18/2010
sinful habits remove for perfection (Jesus)	11/10/2010
soul give thanks, love to angel (Jesus)	12/3/2010
souls of the dead many in purgatory (Jesus)	10/21/2010
souls, keep pure Confession, ready for death (Jesus)	12/7/2010
souls, saving better than losing possessions (Jesus)	10/7/2010
spending control of entitlements, pensions (Jesus)	10/7/2010
spiritual communication by prayers to God (Jesus)	12/21/2010
spiritual life in soul satisfied by peace of Jesus (Jesus)	12/24/2010
springs at refuges healing water (Jesus)	11/26/2010
St. John the Baptist messenger in desert for Jesus (Jesus)	12/23/2010
St. John the Baptist miraculous birth (Jesus)	12/23/2010
St. John the Baptist repent of our sins (Jesus)	12/5/2010
St. John, end times in Book of Revelation (Jesus)	12/27/2010
St. Joseph's mission word of Blessed Mother (Mary)	12/19/2010
St. Peter & St. Paul pillars of the Church (Jesus)	11/18/2010
St. Therese keep peace, not rushed St. Therese"	10/1/2010
St. Therese prayer novena, new DVD St. Therese"	11/1/2010
stage of life actors to use talents (Jesus)	12/31/2010
Star of Bethlehem announces Jesus' birth (Jesus)	12/23/2010
Star of Bethlehem Light disperses the darkness (Jesus)	12/12/2010
Stay awake for Jesus' return (Jesus)	11/28/2010
Sunday Mass attendance down because of lukewarm (Jesus)	11/18/2010
talents accountable for how used (Jesus)	11/17/2010
Tea Party against deficits,lost freedoms (Jesus)	11/4/2010
Tea Party fighting Democrats' lies (Jesus)	10/21/2010
Tea Party smear covers bad voting record (Jesus)	10/28/2010
temptations to sin subtle good, habitual sins (Jesus)	10/19/2010
terrorist attacks around holy days (Jesus)	12/23/2010
terrorist attacks near Christian holy days (Jesus)	12/6/2010
terrorists kill for its own sake (Jesus)	11/29/2010
Thank God by sharing with others (Jesus)	10/10/2010
Thank God for gifts in faith, life, Eucharist (Jesus)	10/10/2010
thanks to God by sharing with the poor (Jesus)	11/25/2010
Thanksgiving for gifts of life in family (Jesus)	11/23/2010
toxic assets held by the government (Jesus)	10/13/2010
tribulation purgatory on earth (Jesus)	10/6/2010
tribulation signs chips, death camps, Antichrist (Jesus)	10/6/2010
tribulation time shortened for sake of elect (Jesus)	12/30/2010
truck deliveries risk with fuel costs,weather (Jesus)	12/18/2010
TV & internet brainwashing people, 1 hr. (Jesus)	12/8/2010
TV, radio censored for political correctness (Jesus)	10/21/2010
underground cities famine,EMP attack,viruses (Jesus)	11/2/2010
underground cities protect VIPs (Jesus)	12/9/2010
underground cities sign of big event coming (Jesus)	11/14/2010
used cars, computers interest to save money (Jesus)	12/16/2010
viruses, deadly to reduce the population (Jesus)	10/15/2010
Wall Street losses protect identity,pray for crooks (Jesus)	10/29/2010
War spending causing deficits,bankruptcy (Jesus)	10/19/2010
Warning wake up call for sinners (Jesus)	10/11/2010
Warning & refuges supernatural intervention (Jesus)	12/16/2010
Warning experience focus on unforgiven sins (Jesus)	12/26/2010
Warning is close by current events on chips (Jesus)	12/2/2010
Warning messages getting close by frequency (Jesus)	12/4/2010
Warning preparation confess unforgiven sins (Jesus)	12/4/2010
Warning result to seek Confession (Jesus)	12/4/2010
water for refuge mechanical pump (Jesus)	11/26/2010
winter time for pandemic virus (Jesus)	12/15/2010
winter preparations store food & fuel (Jesus)	12/13/2010
winter signs test of endurance (Jesus)	11/24/2010
world famine, caused 1 yr. supply of food (Jesus)	11/12/2010

More Messages

If you would like to take advantage of more precious words from Jesus and Mary and apply them to your lives, read the first three volumes of messages and visions given to us through John's special gift. Each book contains a full year of daily messages and visions. As Jesus and Mary said in volume IV:

Listen to My words of warning, and you will be ready to share in the beauty of the Second Coming. Jesus 7/4/96

I will work miracles of conversion on those who read these books with an open mind. Jesus 9/5/96

Prepare for the Great Tribulation and the Era of Peace

Volume I - *July 1993 to June 1994,*
ISBN# 1-882972-69-4, 256pp. $7.95

Volume II - *July 1994 to June 1995,*
ISBN# 1-882972-72-4, 352pp. $8.95

Volume III - *July 1995 to July 10, 1996,*
ISBN# 1-882972-77-5, 384pp. $8.95

Volume IV - *July 11, 1996 to Sept. 30, 1996,*
ISBN# 1-882972-91-0, 104pp. $3.95

Volume V - *Oct. 1, 1996 to Dec. 31, 1996,*
ISBN# 1-882972-97-X, 120pp. $3.95

Volume VI - *Jan. 1, 1997 to Mar. 31, 1997,*
ISBN# 1-57918-002-7, 112pp. $3.95

Volume VII - *April 1, 1997 to June 30, 1997,*
ISBN# 1-57918-010-8, 112pp. $3.95

Volume VIII - *July 1, 1997 to Sept. 30, 1997,*
ISBN# 1-57918-053-1, 128pp. $3.95

Volume IX - *Oct. 1, 1997 to Dec. 31, 1997,*
ISBN# 1-57918-066-3, 168pp. $3.95

Volume X - *Jan. 1, 1998 to Mar. 31, 1998,*
ISBN# 1-57918-073-6, 116pp. $3.95

Volume XI - *Apr. 1, 1998 to June 30, 1998,*
ISBN# 1-57918-096-5, 128pp. $3.95

Volume XII - *July 1, 1998 to Sept. 30, 1998,*
ISBN# 1-57918-105-8, 128pp. $3.95

Volume XIII - *Oct. 1, 1998 to Dec. 31, 1998,*
ISBN# 1-57918-113-9, 134pp. $3.95

Volume XIV - *Jan. 1, 1999 to Mar. 31, 1999,*
ISBN# 1-57918-115-5, 128pp. $3.95

Volume XV - *Apr. 1, 1999 to June 30, 1999,*
ISBN# 1-57918-122-8, 128pp. $3.95

Volume XVI - *July 1, 1999 to Sept. 31, 1999,*
ISBN# 1-57918-126-0, 136pp. $3.95

Volume XVII - *Oct. 1, 1999 to Dec. 31, 1999,*
ISBN# 1-57918-156-2, 136pp. $3.95

Volume XVII - *Jan. 1, 2000 to Mar. 31, 2000,*
ISBN# 1-57918-158-9, 136pp. $3.95

Volume XIX - *Apr. 1, 2000 to June 30, 2000,*
ISBN# 1-57918-160-0, 136pp. $3.95

Volume XX - *July 1, 2000 to Sept. 30, 2000,*
ISBN# 1-57918-162-7, 136pp. $3.95

Volume XXI - *Oct. 1, 2000 to Dec. 31, 2000,*
ISBN# 1-57918-160-0, 136pp. $3.95

Prepare for the Great Tribulation and the Era of Peace

Volume XXII - *Jan. 1, 2001 to Mar. 31, 2001,*
ISBN# 1-57918-172-4, 136pp. $3.95

Volume XXIII - *Apr. 1, 2001 to June 30, 2001,*
ISBN# 1-57918-173-2, 136pp. $3.95

Volume XXIV - *July 1, 2001 to Sept. 30, 2001,*
ISBN# 1-57918-174-0, 136pp. $3.95

Volume XXV - *Oct. 1, 2001 to Dec. 31, 2001,*
ISBN# 1-57918-193-7, 136pp. $3.95

Volume XXVI - *Jan. 1, 2002 to Mar. 31, 2002,*
ISBN# 1-57918-198-1, 136pp. $3.95

Volume XXVII - *Apr. 1, 2002 to June. 30, 2002,*
ISBN# 1-57918-200-3, 136pp. $3.95

Volume XXVIII - *July 1, 2002 to Sept. 30, 2002,*
ISBN# 1-57918-221-6, 136pp.   • $3.95

Volume XXIX - *Oct. 1, 2002 to Dec. 31, 2002,*
ISBN# 1-57918-231-3, 136pp. $3.95

Volume XXX - *Jan. 1, 2003 to Mar. 31, 2003,*
ISBN# 1-57918-235-6, 136pp. $3.95

Volume XXXI - *Apr. 1, 2003 to June. 30, 2003,*
ISBN# 1-57918-240-2, 136pp. $3.95

Volume XXXII - *July 1, 2003 to Sept. 30, 2003,*
ISBN# 1-57918-245-3, 136pp. $3.95

Volume XXXIII - *Oct. 1, 2003 to Dec. 31, 2003,*
ISBN# 1-57918-248-8, 136pp. $3.95

Volume XXXIV - *Jan. 1, 2004 to Mar. 31, 2004,*
ISBN# 1-57918-263-1, 144pp. $3.95

Volume XXXV - *Apr. 1, 2004 to June. 30, 2004,*
ISBN# 1-57918-267-4, 136pp. $3.95

Volume XXXVI - *July 1, 2004 to Sept. 30, 2004,*
ISBN# 1-57918-270-4, 144pp. $4.95

Volume XXXVII - *Oct. 1, 2004 to Dec. 31, 2004,*
ISBN# 1-57918-247-7, 144pp. $4.95

Volume XXXVIII - *Jan. 1, 2005 to Mar. 31,*
2005, ISBN# 1-57918-276-3, 136pp. $4.95

Volume XXXIX - *Apr. 1, 2005 to June. 30, 2005,*
ISBN# 1-57918-288-7, 128pp. $4.95

Volume XXXX - *July 1, 2005 to Sept. 30, 2005,*
ISBN# 1-57918-292-5, 124-pp. $4.95

Volume XLI - *Oct. 1, 2005 to Dec. 31, 2005,*
ISBN# 1-57918-296-8 , 124pp. $4.95

Volume XLII - *Jan. 1, 2006 to Mar. 31, 2006,*
ISBN# 1-57918-299-2, 136pp. $4.95

Volume XLIII - *Apr. 1, 2006 to Jun. 30, 2006,*
ISBN# 1-57918-317-4, 120pp. $4.95

Volume XLIV - *July 1, 2006 to Sept. 30, 2006,*
ISBN# 1-57918-321-2, 124-pp. $4.95

Volume XLV - *Oct. 1, 2006 to Dec. 31, 2006,*
ISBN# 1-57918-324-7, 124pp. $4.95

Volume XLVI - *Jan. 1, 2007 to Mar. 31, 2007,*
ISBN# 1-57918-328-X, 120pp. $4.95

Volume XLVII - *Apr. 1, 2007 to Jun. 30, 2007,*
ISBN# 1-57918-345-X, 124pp. $4.95

Volume XLVIII - *July 1, 2007 to Sept. 30, 2007,*
ISBN# 1-57918-350-6, 128-pp. $4.95

Volume XLIX - *Oct. 1, 2007 to Dec. 31, 2007,*
ISBN# 1-57918-353-0, 120pp. $4.95

Volume L - *Jan. 1, 2008 to Mar. 31, 2008,*
ISBN# 978-1-57918-360-3, 140pp. $4.95

Volume LI - *Apr. 1, 2008 to Jun. 30, 2008,*
ISBN# 978-1-57918-363-8, 124pp. $4.95

Volume LII - *July 1, 2008 to Sept. 30, 2008,*
ISBN# 978-1-57918-367-0, 124pp. $4.95

Volume LIII - *Oct. 1, 2008 to Dec. 31, 2008,*
ISBN# 978-1-57918-371-9, 130pp. $4.95

Volume LIV - *Jan. 1, 2009 to Mar. 31, 2009,*
ISBN# 978-1-57918-373-5, 120pp. $4.95

Volume LV - *Apr. 1, 2009 to Jun. 30, 2009,*
ISBN# 978-1-57918-376-X, 124pp. $4.95

Volume LVI - *July 1, 2009 to Sept. 30, 2009,*
ISBN# 978-1-57918-380-8, 116pp. $4.95

Volume LVII - *Oct. 1, 2009 to Dec. 31, 2009,*
ISBN# 978-1-57918-384-0, 124pp. $5.95

Volume LVIII - *Jan. 1, 2010 to Mar. 31, 2010,*
ISBN# 978-1-57918-386-7, 128pp. $5.95

Volume LIX - *Apr. 1, 2010 to Jun. 30, 2010,*
ISBN# 978-1-57918-393-X, 132pp. $5.95

Volume LX - *July 1, 2010 to Sept. 30, 2010,*
ISBN# 978-1-57918-398-0, 142pp. $5.95

Volume LXI - *Oct. 1, 2010 to Dec. 31, 2010,*
ISBN# 978-1-57918-401-4, 118pp. $5.95